BEYOND THE DARK ROOM

AN INTERNATIONAL COLLECTION OF TRANSFORMATIVE POETRY

EDITED BY DR. PEARL KETOVER PRILIK

RLYB

Beyond The Dark Room
An International Collection of Transformative Poetry

First Edition published 2012
by ReallyLoveYourBook
Unit 11, Concord House, Main Avenue, Bridgend, UK. CF31 2AG
www.reallyloveyourbook.com

ISBN   978-1-907375-75-0

Edited by Dr. Pearl Ketover Prilik
Cover photograph © 2012 Jane Penland Hoover
Cover design © 2012 Rob Halpin

1 3 5 7 9 10 8 6 4 2

British Library Cataloguing in Publication Data.
A catalogue record for this book is available from the British Library.

Printed in the UK by Lightning Source, Milton Keynes.

Introduction

By Dr. Pearl Ketover Prilik

"People are like stained - glass windows. They sparkle and shine when the sun is out, but when the darkness sets in, their true beauty is revealed only if there is a light from within."

Elisabeth Kubler-Ross

Human beings possess a wondrous capacity to survive. This ability to move beyond life's challenges and, or if need be, to fashion a life where one lives comfortably side by side with them is the heart and spirit of the poems in this collection. The particulars of the continuum of human challenges are often perceived as too brutal to be conceptualized as a "pleasurable read." Yet the transcendence found in the darkest of places is illuminated by the poetic need to articulate what might otherwise remain unspeakable. Poetry is perhaps the best vehicle to ride the majestic human journey from betrayal, through trauma and onward toward healing and love. The poets and poems that you will find in the pages of this volume passionately describe these passages. It is my deeply held belief, that one's ability to continue not only to "survive" and "cope" but to move beyond pain to enjoy a lived-life of love, joy and trust lit from within, is the poem of humanity itself.

This notion of "light" or an inner "spark" is obviously not new – in fact a great deal of religious, spiritual and philosophical thought is devoted to such musings.

I do believe that this light or spark and the concurrent ability to move beyond adversity, lies at the very core of the human experience itself. The world is filled with wonders: physical, psychological and meta-physical. Throughout the ages, poets have acted as documentarians expressing their irrepressible passion to record and share experiences both in the tangible physical sense, and in that meta-physical felt-world within. Yet, for all the marvels that a poet might rhapsodize about I have found none greater than the human capacity to survive and to thrive. The world's wonders feed the poets' desire to document and to make sense of human experience, most compellingly in this volume is the awe inspiring capacity to enjoy the beauty in life after experiencing its ugliness. And, so this anthology's title and the poems themselves honor the passage through the stages of survival to the "beyond" of healing.

In the yin and yang, the here and now, the balanced nature of all things, where there is light there will inevitably be dark. This is the "Dark Room" of the title,
chosen to describe the psychic or actual places and situations where individuals or groups find themselves potentially trapped by insurmountable challenges or the imprisonment of personal or collective cultures or belief systems that seek to strip dignity and threaten the full flowering of selfhood.

However, it is important to honor a different perspective: Where for some dark rooms signify entrapment, for many others dark rooms signify places of introspective contemplation, perhaps borne of challenges, places in where one can deal with and make meaning of the best and worst of human experience. A photographer might accurately point out that all photographs require both light and dark - too much of either one distorts the picture. And so, dark rooms themselves can be beacons pointing to the light of discovery and creation.

Obviously, neither an individual nor a group moves easily from a place of struggle and pain to enjoying a fulfilled life. Such a voyage has a meandering emotional quality. Some of the most common of these points along the way involve particular emotions, which became the ten chapter headings: stunned, anger, fear, shock, depression, empowerment, calm, trust, confidence, and a feeling of love, fulfillment and even peace. The ten chapters of this anthology are divided evenly between emotions that address painful and reparative portions of this ride.

In no way is Beyond The Dark Room describing a linear voyage: In the way of life and poetry such stages often fold one onto the other and are only experienced or observed as a shimmering "beyond" that is not an endpoint but rather a coalescence of shifting senses and integration of experiences or:

If I were to condense this introduction to a single sentence it would be : Human beings suffer and transcend suffering, an experience poets use to make meaning of what it is to be alive. These poems address the passage from pain to transcendence ---
                    Jane Shlensky

The original idea for this anthology was tossed out as an idea on a social page for a collection that would speak to the horrific issue of betrayal of trust inherent in child abuse – it was intended as an honorific to children so assaulted and to the adults they grow to become. I began to think that in order for a child's trust to be "betrayed" there is an implication that "trust," or at the very least, the capacity to trust, may very well be an innate quality with which each infant is born. Perhaps then, this magnificent quality to survive and thrive, going *beyond* the ability to endure, hardship, adversity, abuse, challenges, war, devastation, hunger; the entire spectrum of possible human pain, lies somewhere in a hard-wired and inextinguishable trust in life itself. Perhaps it is this sense of positive trust that illuminates and continues to burn, extraordinarily brightly within some individuals, despite all attempts to extinguish.

This collection speaks to extraordinarily large questions: How does one stumble in starvation from the horrors of concentration camps and laugh again? How does one suffer at the hand of a loved one turned in pain and perversion and offer oneself willingly to another's love? How does one whose eyes have been filled with the blood of war return home to live in laughing peace? Kick a dog or a cat, and that animal will live a legacy of fear. Yet, somehow some, people have an incredible capacity to endure, thrive, and move "beyond" their individual and collective so-called "dark rooms." How? The answer to such a question is neither simple, nor straight-forward; it is here where poetry is perhaps best suited as both a vehicle in which one may ride this journey and an expression of the experience itself.

The poets within this collection have been moved by challenges to self, and others – each writing with his or her own unique clear voice. Each poem in this collection stands alone as a shimmering work of art – all poems gathered together are a chorus composed of the spirited resilience of humanity. We are all known to one another in that particularly intimate sense that the virtual reality of the Internet so uniquely provides. Our reach extends across the United States over the border of Canada and across the seas to the UK and to Australia. Many of the poets in this collection have been writing and reading each other's works for five years or longer on various poetic sites. This collection was a particularly gentle and delightful collaboration, with a host of exquisite photographs submitted by some of our poet/photographers for cover consideration choices voted upon. There was a particular ease and collaborative spirit involved in this process as though the process of gathering this anthology together was illuminated by the very sense of resilience and capacity for enjoyment to which the included poems speak.

It has been a wonderful process from beginning to conclusion; this introduction cannot end without a few most heart-felt special mentions: Jane Shlensky who has both patiently proofed my proofing and made suggestions in an attempt to bring clarity to this introduction which I fear would have been a rambling free verse without her steady eye. Pamela Smyk Clearly who collected photographs and created mock-up covers. Jane Penland Hoover whose exquisite photograph is our anthology's cover and represents the sense of this collection as moving beyond a room out into a garden of potential and existent joyful color. Jane Shlensky and S.E. Ingraham, kindly provided much appreciated opinions and support. Rob Halpin, our cover designer – a wonderful team player who stepped in with creativity and patience and brought color and life to our cover. Laura Hegfield who brought this collection to the attention of some wonderfully talented people, who generously shared their enjoyment of and support for our project.

A special thank you to Dr. Nurit Nora Israeli for her Foreword where she beautifully intermingles her philosophical, professional and personal views of moving beyond in a manner that perfectly reflects the spirit of this anthology. Finally, I want to offer a wealth of gratitude once again to each and every poet in this collection who took the time to be part of this project, to vote on various aspects of its presentation and to carefully proof their own work. Any errors that have escaped and are noticed after publication will be my responsibility completely – as a group I do believe that we have coalesced as a collaborative, connected voice supporting, contrasting and harmonizing with one another as we visited one another's dark rooms and together moved to 'beyond.' It remains my honor to be a part of this effort and we all hope that you enjoy the poems that have been collected for that purpose.

In our personal sense of social justice and in the global human spirit of how humanity can gather and make a more compassionate world, all royalties will be donated to Doctors Without Borders/Médecins Sans Frontières (MSF), an international medical humanitarian organization created by doctors and journalists in France in 1971. To read more about this organization visit
http://doctorswithoutborders.org/

Foreword
By Dr. Nurit Nora Israeli

When I found out that an anthology of poems was going to
be published titled "Beyond the Dark Room..." – my heart
skipped a beat, as this particular title reflects major themes
in both my personal and professional lives. I read the
anthology and felt as though I was entering a very familiar
room, where the interplay between the darkness and light
inherent in any transformational journey was beautifully
reflected.

In my professional role as a psychologist, I have been
privileged to bear witness to the uniqueness with which
individuals move in and out of 'dark rooms', and how these
journeys radically transform them.   I have dedicated much
of my professional life to studying the impact of trauma, the
grieving process, and – more recently – Posttraumatic
Growth, as well as ways of integrating a spiritual
perspective in the practice of Psychology.   My work has
focused on different dimensions of Living With and Beyond
Loss.

My personal sense of moving beyond the 'dark room' is best
depicted by my poem, which reflects my experience with
radiation for breast cancer and the healing process that
followed, and which, serendipitously, brought me to this
anthology:

IN AND OUT OF THE DARK ROOM
(Or: SURRENDER –IN TWO ACTS)

BY: DR. NURIT ISRAELI

I. RADIATION

Lying flat on my back
Under the ominous machine –
My body arranged by others,
Locked in a cast,
Abandoned in the cold dark room.
Lying motionless, like a corpse,
Day after day:
Waiting for the beams
To attack rebellious cells;
And on the way to salvation –
Feeling the fire of hell
Mark my soul
With third degree burns…

II. FLOATING IN ANTIGUA

Lying flat on my back
Under the bluest of skies,
Caressed by the soft light
Of the early morning sun,
Cuddled by the warm Caribbean water,
Surrendering to the waves,
Letting go,
Day after day:
Floating away from landscapes of pain,
Spilling chunks of bad memories
To be swept away –
Replaced by new imprints
Of peace and hope;
Trusting the sea to fade my scars,
Hearing, again, the heartbeat of life
In the depth of its silence.

I was born in the midst of World War II, in the shadow of the Holocaust, to parents whose legacy was: *"In spite of everything – YES!"* I was born in the midst of my parents' grieving losses, born into the midst of their pain and suffering. Life vacillated between the darkness of the outside world and the light I had to create from within to brighten the lives of those around me, as well as my own. I tried to live fully – for all my ancestors who could not.

My father refused to name me after his beloved mother, whom he adored, because she had died of breast cancer, and he did not want to 'expose' me to it. Yet, he did repeatedly tell me how similar I was to my grandmother, and how connected she and I could have been. I was not surprised when I discovered that I was 'following her footsteps,' diagnosed with a breast cancer in 2005 and a recurrence in 2008.

Initially, I felt overwhelmed. I did not want to cross that imaginary line from 'health' to 'illness', to enter a world where life and death are closely intertwined. I went through an intense grieving process, and writing became a major vehicle for introspection, exploration, and discovery. It helped me search for meaning within trauma, regain some of the control which I had lost, and re-assess my life. Through it, I got in touch with both, my vulnerabilities and my strengths.

In this new personal 'dark room', I recalled and relied upon earlier experiences of coping with challenging circumstances. When I first came to NY, I dreaded the cold winters. I would walk outdoors all constricted, my muscles tensed and my head buried in my shoulders -- trying to defend myself against the blowing winds. After several years and advice from a wise friend, I realized that I need to embrace the cold, walk through it, allowing the blood to flow freely in my veins to warm me up. I attempted to apply that lesson to this new 'cold wave' -- trying to embrace the inevitable with open arms and an open heart.

Writing helped me face the storm and navigate my way through it. Many years ago, while learning to swim in the beautiful beach of my hometown, I was taught that when a tidal wave comes my way -- I should never try to escape. Rather, I should face it and dive under it, floating with the current -- so that I would emerge on the other side unharmed. I remembered the feeling of being 'on the other side of the wave' -- the sense of well being in a sea that turns calm, with the threatening wave moving away, becoming smaller and smaller. Now again, I was trying to 'float with the current' on my way to a calmer sea. I began to look forward to the rainbow that follows a storm -- knowing that I would enjoy its bright colors like never before.

In making my own way through personal 'dark rooms', I moved in the direction of the light. Along the way, I learned to live 'deeper' rather than 'wider'. I learned to accept the 'legitimacy' of losses, as well as the inevitability of pain and suffering. I also learned to acknowledge death as a viable force -- unreasonable, non-negotiable, unfair, and uncontrollable. The fact that I held on to the belief that I will come out of this crisis did not erase the raw suffering, and I allowed myself to feel it all -- denying nothing.

My initial goal was survival, but my journey has taken me far beyond. I remain in love with life. I continue to celebrate with abandon life's shining glitters: my family, my friends, nature, and the ample opportunities presented by each new day. I love to dance, and when I dance now, I can literally hear my heart beat -- feeling intense gratitude for being healthy, intense pleasure in being alive.

I have a new ritual: Every year for my birthday I go to the beach, taking along some mementos that represent the passing year. First, I allow myself to grieve – cathartically. I grieve not only for my own losses, but also for the pain around me – for those in hospitals all over fighting for their lives, bearing sometimes unbearable pain, for the victims of wars and cruelty, poverty, and loneliness. I grieve for the unfairness and for the indifference, for the fragility and vulnerability, for the shortness of our days in this troubled yet wonderful planet. Then, I celebrate with loved ones, toasting life, feeling grateful – looking forward to the next chapter. In whatever time I have left, I intend to live fully. I will continue to build my 'sand castles' with passion and care, while remaining fully aware of the coming tide.

I would like to say a few words directly to the readers of this anthology: If you chose to enter the 'dark rooms' depicted here, you are a fellow seeker on the path -- searching for your own unique way of embracing the cold. I have some wishes for you as you proceed to meet or reflect upon the challenges of your own journey:

First, I wish you clarity of purpose – the ability to focus on what really matters to you. A patient who suffered a major loss this past year told me that, as a result, he is concerned less about his 'success', more about his relationships; spending more time outdoors smelling the flowers; finding comfort in nature, in poetry, in music; trying harder not to sweat the small stuff.

I wish that you remain passionately involved in the things that are of importance, interest, and concern to you. Continue to pay close attention to whatever you treasure, especially relationships with those dear to you. Keep on opening up to people, let your true self touch theirs, so you can feel your common humanity. Continue to reach out to others with empathy and compassion. Generosity, kindness, and – above all – love are the most important bridges that connect us. At the same time, accept your vulnerability and do not hesitate to ask for help when you need it: As we all know, helping is very gratifying for the helper. Be kind to yourself. Learn to forgive yourself, so you can forgive others. Forgiveness can lessen bitterness, diminish guilt, and introduce hope.

In my recent presentation "Living With and Beyond Loss," I spoke about the "small cemeteries which lie deep in each of our hearts – cemeteries where dreams and plans and hopes are buried." So many of the scripts we write for ourselves prove to be unattainable, inaccessible, unreachable. The older we become, the more losses we sustain, so grieving our inevitable losses is an important part of living. Aspire to meet difficulties with courage and with dignity. It is not easy to do, but it is an important goal.

Pursue your own spiritual journey. Your search is your own. However, you may find comfort walking side-by-side

with others pursuing similar journeys.   Embrace life. Keep
on growing.   Continue your search for meaning.   Explore
new pathways.   Remember Viktor Frankl's guiding motto,
borrowed from Nietzsche, in Man's Search for Meaning:
"He who has a Why to live can bear with almost any How."
Hold on to your ultimate freedom – the freedom to find
meaning and purpose.   Find meaning in both your joys and
your sorrows.   See the extraordinary in the ordinary.
Remain open to new possibilities.

What is the most important lesson life has taught me?   It is
that we do have to go through 'dark rooms':   hardships and
misfortunes do present themselves on the course of our
lives, but they bring with them great opportunities to learn
what most matters to us.   Remember: shining stars are
only visible in the darkness.   Try to recognize,
acknowledge, and be grateful for what you do have and for
what can still be.   Let the guiding motto of the next chapter
of your life be: "*In spite of everything -- yes!*"

In summary, this very special anthology is an invitation to
bear witness to both the positive and the negative
dimensions of the journey through life's challenges.   The
poems are an inspiring testament to the interface between
the vulnerabilities and the resilience of the human spirit,
and to the potential for growth inherent even in the most
adverse circumstances.   Entering the 'rooms' so intimately
and sensitively depicted in this anthology is likely to take
you, the reader, to the shadows and lights in your personal
'rooms' -- inviting you to reflect upon your own ways of
facing darkness, and of mustering the hope and the courage
necessary to keep moving in the direction of the light.

*Dr. Nurit Nora Israeli received her doctorate in Psychology
from Columbia University - Teachers College. Teaching and
training have been a major focus of Dr. Israeli's career.
She has been the Director of Child and Family Therapy &
Coordinator of Psychology Training, Pederson-Krag Center,
Huntington, NY; an Adjunct Associate Professor of
Psychology at Columbia University - Teachers College,
Faculty and Supervisor at the Postdoctoral Program in
Couple Therapy, Adelphi University; and a member of the*

Committee of Accreditation of Postdoctoral training Programs in Family Psychology, American Psychological Association, Division of Family Psychology. Her private practice of Psychology has been in Jericho, NY. Dr. Israeli's clinical work as well as her courses, workshops, and presentations have focused on the therapeutic uses of expressive and reflective writing across the life span to promote personal growth and emotional well-being.

Dedicated to the poets of these pages
who have passionately illuminated the journey
of all who reach out *beyond*.

Sitting in the Dark
an introductory poem
Jane Shlensky

Sunday afternoons—while we kids visited
our friends or went to Uncle John's with Dad
to escape a farm rife with home-grown boredom—
were hers to do with as she liked, alone.

Perhaps she read or took a nap,
or wrote another poem or cried as a release.
Maybe she played a few old hymns on piano,
or sang wistful songs in her wispy soprano.

We only know that when we came back
in time to milk the cows, we found her in the den
sitting in silence as evening fell and shadows
took the room, slate-gray evenings with the last

rays of sunlight fierce, shooting pinks and oranges
across the sky beyond the fields. She sat in gathering
darkness and then in night itself, where we found her
and whispered to one another, "What's wrong with her?"

and to her, "Mama, don't you want the light on?"
Speaking was an effort, breaking some spell she valued,
maybe more than us. She was past words and glad.
"No. Go away until you understand," she said,

sending us to milk the cows in twilight,
our cheeks against their warm flanks,
their raspy tongues licking at their feed
and the rhythm of milk hitting the pails,

cats begging nearby, the barnyard smelling of warmth,
mellow hay, and silage, darkness carrying the scent
of rest from labor and thankfulness after full day.
We milked, wordless, drinking in something of home.

We could have gone away forever, never understood,
but aging and living have seated us in our own dark
rooms, letting a new light reshape us, counsel us,
humble and free us, wondering if we've got it yet.

We do not know what she felt watching day reach
to embrace the night, the kindness of the unseen
revealing itself to her changed vision. We sit in our own
rooms now, remembering, settling into dusky peace, moved.

Contents

1. STUNNED

You tell yourself -it's none of your business -until you see the paramedics- roll one of them out- under a white sheet.
Rob Halpin – Apathy

flattened by-the express train-that is-you.
Diana Terrill Clark – Flattened

Dark Room
Michael Grove

She sat inside her dark room
and gazed outward at the light.
She wished and hoped and dreamed
that someday soon she might
step outside of her dark room
and find happiness somewhere
so she could heal her scars
and live life without a care.
I guess she'd rather feel the pain
and wait right there to die
so she sat inside her dark room
and watched the world go by.

Apathy
Rob Halpin

The haughty lady down the hall
always wears shades,
cakes on make-up, and
cringes, turns away when you
begin to say hello.
The spastic child
who's always got bruises
claims he broke his arm
skateboarding, but
you've never seen him outside.
You tell yourself
it's none of your business
until you see the paramedics
roll one of them out
under a white sheet.

For all the times that might have been the last time

Marian J. Veverka

The thunder had diminished to a low mutter and
You said "I think the rain is over" and you
Picked up your jacket and I watched your arms
As they slid into the sleeves and I said
"I'll walk out with you."
Or maybe I didn't say it out loud, but it
Was what I thought.
So we walked together to the driveway
And I watched as you brushed away
Some leaves and twigs that had
Fallen on your windshield and
The air still smelled like rain, there
Were puddles everywhere --I think
Our feet got wet, I'm not sure
Because I didn't know that this would be
The last time.
I mean, I knew you were upset and I was,
Too, but I didn't cry, not then, I didn't
Want to cause a scene and I thought we could
Talk about it later on maybe tomorrow or some
Other time, because I believed that
There would always be more time. So
You slid into the drivers seat and closed
The door and I leaned over to kiss you through
The window but it was closed. And you turned
On the ignition and the lights and began to
Back out of the drive and all I could do was
Wave and call "Good-bye! Good-bye!"

When you turned into the road, your tail
Lights left narrow streaks of red on the
Wet pavement and I waved again as you
Picked up speed
"Good-bye, good-bye"
I remember the sound of the water running down
The drain from the eaves and the splashing of
Other cars as they drove past and I took deep
Breaths because the air was fresh and smelled of water
And I didn't want to cry.

Originally published in "Up the Staircase" Spring 2009 issue

Instructions

ina Roy-Faderman

Store yourself
in the ice box
to prevent bruising
and corruption.
If scars appear
from the pressure of the shelf,
if the skin is
broken -
still, flies cannot
lay in you their eggs,
still, you can live out
your time,
still, the flesh
underneath can remain
sweet and undisturbed.

Dishonored

J.lynn Sheridan

If you sharpen a spike on a wooden cross
and drive it into my stomach, it will hurt
the first time,
the second even.

The third time, I will gasp and spit,
but feel nothing even though the pain
will spark like white hot coals.
I'll see nothing and you will
no longer matter.

Charred ashes remain in a pit, but sparks rise to join
the Father of heavenly lights.

Constancy

Jane Shlensky

I have a friend who betrays me.
Often and willfully, she breaks
my heart and challenges my trust
in her and my faith in myself.

And it hurts every time I say
I have a friend who betrays me,
for what sort of friend is that,
to lie and abuse those who love her?

But somehow I'm engaged by this
constancy of forgiveness, of doubt.
I have a friend who betrays me,
whom I can't forget, whom I love.

These words come from a sad place
in me, for I don't crave abuse,
and yet I want to honor truth:
I have a friend who betrays me.

At 31 After His Heart-Valve Surgery

Jane Penland Hoover

My twelve-hour wait ended
"You may go in for ten minutes."

All five feet three inches of me,
thanks to four-inch heels,
clicked down the hall and into his room.
I expected to give him a big smile
say, "Well, how are YOU doing?"

Barely into the room
the door closed behind me.
Everything stopped.
Nothing anyone had said
prepared me for seeing him
motionless
tubes and wires threading through
connecting him
to machines, pumps, and other things –
I didn't want to know.

If I moved closer,
could I touch him?

I stood three feet from the bed,
"Ron... Ron..."

He gave no response.
The noise — breathing machine
pulsing – pushing — swoosh –
– air into lungs — pause –
whoosh – sucking out –
again – swoosh.
His chest rose and fell
to the will of the machine.

In this gripping rhythm
I began synchronizing
my breath to his
– in – out – in – out –
– anything – to
– remain connected
not allow this separation.

Bitter Reflection

Patricia A. Hawkenson

At first only the wind
then the bitter sting
of sleet
till the air gasped
and the crystals fluffed
with one alone
to melt upon my tongue.

The field in time transformed
and I overwhelmed
in white
wondering
from where the first word
came to land
and where the rest
piled up.

Flattened

Diana Terrill Clark

We lived on a dead-end
street
with railroad tracks
beyond the railing.

We would put pennies
(and even quarters
when we were feeling rich)
on the tracks and wait for a train
to come
and mash the coin
flinging it off
to the side.

We would hunt for the coins
and crow
when we found one
flattened beyond
recognition.

Now I feel like one of those
formerly useful
coins,
flattened by
the express train
that is
you.

2. ANGER

Jagged pieces crumbling slow to the ground, - your face was smooth again except for the scowl. - Your knuckles, though, still raised, were bloody.

Rosemary Nissen-Wade – Violence

Anger, oh my foe, my friend, - how is it you so move me? - It is not a dance I enjoy.

Richard Walker – An Angry Pantoum

Welcome to the Jungle

S.E. Ingraham

They found him behind a dumpster near the Mustard Seed Church
Somebody had beaten the crap out of him, maybe more than one somebodies
His handsome face, unrecognizable, save maybe for the tear tattoo 'neath his right
eye
He had blood encrusted around his nose and mouth, both eyes swollen shut,
And a cut at his hairline looked deep, more of a gash really, it ran into his thick hair,
Got lost somewhere back there, probably near the crown where there was matting
An unnatural flattening of thick native hair, black and shining, quickly losing its
lustre
While he lay there in the trash as if he too, were garbage, a throw-away, soon
forgotten

Was this part of the famous aboriginal gang violence we keep hearing about?
Another Warrior vengeance killing? Or was something else at play here...
The native kids usually cut each other but they weren't much into fist play
Didn't seem to punch the living daylights out of anybody - plus, this poor guy had
A special humiliation accorded him that seemed like payback of a different kind
Around his neck, someone had fashioned a crude sign, almost too articulate for what
it was;
it read:
"Remember Guns 'N Roses LOSER? They Be Gone -
They may be back. But not you LOSER"

Heavy emphasis on the word "LOSER". Trying to make a point? Just
unimaginative?
Hard to say, I think, as the coroner's staff loads the body into the back of their van.
Good chance this would be another unclaimed body, another John Doeskin off the
reserve
Buried in that pitiful potter's field; no-one would even know to miss him, I guessed
No-one to come get his poor battered body either, of course.

This job can get to you if you let it, I think, and let my partner finish up the paper-work

As we pull away from the scene, then crank the radio just as "Sweet Child of Mine" starts.

Ironic.

This poem placed third in the "Spirituality" category of Expressions of Hunger, the 2011 City of Edmonton and the Edmonton Food Bank competition. After receiving the award at City Hall, the poem was framed professionally and hung there for several weeks, then subsequently in various art galleries in the city, before being returned to the poet, after several months.

And my thin skin weeps

J.lynn Sheridan

I watch with eyes of teeth,
door-slamming voices, tingling feet,
razor-sharp gnawing, shivering bed aglow,
and my thin skin wilts from weeping for you.

Five-thousand times I have given
red release to you, pounding thumb-cracking
musky taunts that wilt my skin from weeping.

I long to slither between the limp
black oak limbs slumped against
the snow mounds, they smile at

me outside fogged windows,
behind bruised tapestry curtains
that never flutter.

If you would but try, it is possible
to blossom in ice while my thin
skin weeps.

If you would but try.

Condemned to Love

Meena Rose

Contained silence;
Stiff upper lip;
Standing rigidly;
Glowering impassively.

Your look of
Anger,
Disgust,
And Confusion;
Baffle me to this day.

Your voice growing louder;
Condemnation coming through;
You kept demanding,
How could I do this to you?

Let's review the facts here,
Spinster, you did not want me;
You clearly told me to "settle" down,
If I could not, you would force me
To marry one of your friends' sons.

Control of my life you have had plenty;
This notion of yours was totally unfair;
I had to strip you of your power.

So I raced around maddeningly,
Trying to find the ONE,
Before your crazy deadline.

I simply came here to tell you,
That I found the ONE.
It will be him with or without you.

Seriously now, Dad,
What does it matter that he is not a Muslim?

Anger

Barbara Ehrentreu

It builds slowly
like a far away wave
rolling forth
gaining momentum
as the thoughts crowd
her brain
Cresting to its full strength
a force unchecked
and she surveys the damage,
the surf bubbles subsiding
The cuts on her thigh
left behind
like furrows in wet sand
at low tide.

I wasn't there

Jay Sizemore

but I was there...
trapped in the body
of an eight-year-old child,
my short fingers capable
of sending my toys
to imaginary graves,
but not stopping
the tears from streaming
down my mother's face,
not stopping the faceless
fist from tangling
in her long blonde curls
and dragging her from my room
and down the hall.

I can still hear her screaming.

I can still hear the voice
of the monster
calling her bitch,
telling her he is going to
get out his knife,
he is going to
cut the baby out of her guts,
telling her she will never
leave him again.
I can still hear the thud
of his fist in the wall
and the struggle as she fights her way
back out of the darkness.

Moonlight falling in through
the rectangular windows
of this small trailer in the Kentucky woods,
my sister and I curled under the blankets
of our separate bunks and held our breath,
our immature minds incapable of knowing
that we could be hearing
the sounds of
our mother about to die.

But the light came on,
and with a flurry of shouts
and sobs we were in the truck
and gone,
leaving the demon
alone to destroy
everything that could be broken.

I was too young.
I couldn't say
don't go back,
I didn't know my sister's innocence
was under attack,
I didn't know the words "abuse,"
"sexual," or "victim,"
but I felt deep down
a sense of wrong.

I'll never understand why she did it,
believed his apologies and lies,
left me for a year
to live with my grandparents,
while they moved back
into a different trailer
in a different town,
why he was allowed
to hold my baby brother
in his tainted hands.
I wasn't there
but I was.

I'm sorry I wasn't old enough
to know how to load a gun.

Carbolic

ina Roy-Faderman

Pour it
in the wound and watch it
smoke.

Angry Birds
Patricia A. Hawkenson

Cobalt tears seemed to seep
from the crows of my eyes
like water running
on the parched earthen furrows
that were too hardened
to allow the healing moisture in
and days had to pass
before a seed of hope
could rise to greet the sun.

Homecoming

Daniel Ari

I've been edging toward your return since last Saturday.
There's no question that serving as you have is selfless
in a way. When you flew out in 08 to put your life
on the line for this country and its changing ideals,
Katelyn, God bless her, hardly knew that you had gone.
But she grew to feel it. From me, perhaps. I can't reckon
if the emails and videos and Iraqi Xmas gifts helped her
touch your presence or your long absence. Anyway
I told you how she salutes each and every American flag,
the ones in the neighborhood and the one at the mall.
Believe it or not, she's turned six and grown so tall
and graceful. She's pushing her boundaries, says her mom
is on her side, it doesn't matter if she's so far away.
You know, she can read most of the Berenstein Bears
by herself. Did I tell you? Our pastor and our flock
have changed minds about things I thought were certain.
I hardly know anymore what to tell Kate is really real.
Now here you are in your kitchen again with your hubby.
Anyway, I don't know where to start to confess
about what's gone through me since you were away.

Violence

Rosemary Nissen-Wade

You were glaring through the window
when your face broke like crazy paving.
Zig-zag lines and angles fragmented the planes,
just missing your eyes and your nostrils
but cutting across your lips and severing both ears.

Then, as the glass shattered and fell,
jagged pieces crumbling slow to the ground,
your face was smooth again except for the scowl.
Your knuckles, though, still raised, were bloody.

Bitterroot
Diana Terrill Clark

As your daughter,
I wanted to be
part of your life.

Of course I did,
I loved you.

But you were full of fear
or pain
that you hid behind,
telling us kids:
"It hurts too much to see you,
and not get to keep you."

I try to imagine your pain.

How can it compare with
the pain of a child
with no anchor?

No father in the audience
at recitals and plays.

No father at home wanting
to interview her dates.

No father for the
father/daughter dance
at her wedding?

Instead,
I find myself
on the sidelines.
Hearing about you from others;
witnesses to your life.
They know you,
I don't.

I hear them say,
"Wow, you look just like your dad!"
and
"He loved you so much."

Really? How can you tell?
I want to yell at them,
scream that he was not the man
they thought he was,
the man who raised my
stepmother's children
so lovingly.

An Angry Pantoum

Richard Walker

Anger, oh my foe, my friend,
how is it you so move me?
It is not a dance I enjoy.
Why are you with me still?

How is it you so move me
to actions of shame and courage?
Why are you with me still
though I have worked to be rid of you?

To actions of shame and courage,
two-faced, you have spurred me on.
Though I have worked to be rid of you,
yet you cling to my fragile heart.

Two-faced, you have spurred me on,
when you should have - and not.
Yet you cling to my fragile heart,
Anger, oh my foe, my friend.

3. FEAR

I smell his cigarette breath - as he leans in to whisper,- "You want some too, boy?"-

                Jay Sizemore – The Bad Dream

sitting in the laundry basket - fingers in my ears- shut the closet- door.

                Patricia A. Hawkenson – Monster in My Closet

trying to fly - certain of success- while she - frozen at the portal

                Pamela Smyk Cleary – Fear Less

Please, God, not again
Rob Halpin

the pop-hiss
of can after can;
foreboding
overture
to the shuffle-step stumble
coming down the hall

Knotted
Laura Hegfield

knotted
constricted
bound by ropes
loosened when seen
for what they truly are
the trappings of mind coiling
'round itself in fear of that which
cannot be constrained, controlled, tamed
courage: sitting in the tangled messiness of life
feeling afraid, doing what needs to be done anyway
trusting that no mind-state is permanent, release is a breath

~~~~~~~~~~~~~~~~~away

In the Shadows

S.E. Ingraham

Even deep in the recesses
Of the basement
Behind the unpacked
Boxes of books
Where the light is dim
And I find myself deep
In shadow;
Reading old journals
Is a masochistic act—
Is like pushing
Splinters of glass
Under my nails—
Is like pulling
My memory bank open
And flashing a klieg light
Inside every corner
Until every tormented line
Reveals itself anew;
Every hurt rises up
To slap me hard
Again ... and again

Door

ina Roy-Faderman

Slam.
You're it.

Stranded

Jane Penland Hoover

On and on in all directions
palmetto, sand, and slash pines stretch,
long shadows fall behind
the way we've come.

Earlier my ocean fervor
imagined all of us refreshed,
by the sea's salt flavored air.

My man weak from surgery.
paralyzed and silenced by the stroke,
still he'd smiled and nodded yes
when I asked, "Ride?"

Edgy, one thumb extended now, I
stand the length of desolation
begging to be helped, taken.
A camper driver brakes.

I run from our stalled car – look back
at the four of them:
he in silence stares,
Grandma cuddles our curly-headed infant,
while five-year old big sister
presses face to pane, pleads, Mom...

Riding east for miles and miles,
I measured minutes, some desire
to flee responsibilities, my world
waiting for a wrecker.

I remember that mechanic,
patient with the damaged parts,
those rescuers trailing lights,
me left alone,
us to navigate the rest.

Dear Bogeyman

Rosemary Nissen-Wade

You missed! I got away
time after time after time,
leaping on the bed
from the middle of the floor,
flying in a flurry
of cotton nightgown,
to land soft and safe
from your sneaky hands
that reached to grab
my naked ankles
and pull me down
into the darkness
of your nether regions.

I never met you in the flesh
though some of my friends did.
I wonder now about those tales,
that fear — where did it come from?
Did fear or tales come first?
Are both an age-old way
of keeping children safe
from real-live bogeymen
who really lie in wait
for unwary children, and who
might even be in your own house,
hiding, ready to pounce,
under your own bed?

Overcome Your Fear

Michael Grove

You were going to do it yesterday.
Might get to it tomorrow.
Perhaps it will still be undone next year.
You think about it all the time.
Project the ideal plan.
The first step is to overcome your fear.

You want to do it perfectly.
You cannot stand to fail.
That's something you detest and sorely dread.
It's better that you move beyond
the fear of second rate.
Sometimes it's simply best to forge ahead.

The first step is the hardest.
The final one, a breeze.
Move beyond obstacles that cloud your mind.
Take a chance and get it done.
Think positively now,
and leave all of your dreaded fears behind.

Fear Less

Pamela Smyk Cleary

Fearless
(she thinks them)
running barefoot on the lawn
spinning in the rain
open arms & eyes & hearts
unafraid to
test their wings
trying to fly
certain of success
while she
frozen at the portal
umbrella in hand
watches
wistfully

His awful frustration

Daniel Ari

When the storm decides to subside
we could celebrate your birthday.
It blew past as we were screaming
in the shelter of the cellar.

We could come out for a picnic
when the storm decides to subside.
As long as we talk quietly,
we can confirm our survival.

The weather presides over us
like an injured father who calms
when the storm decides to subside.
We try to steer it, help it choose

empty skies and the stillest air.
It could be a butterfly wing
or a whimper that determines
when the storm decides to subside.

"I am sorry about my fear"
Richard Walker

I am sorry about my fear
it was my mind's way
of avoiding pain

I know you loved me
you asked me to stay
that made me want to leave

I loved the feel of your
body beneath mine
it was always best

in the morning, the sun
on your skin, the bottles
of Speakeasy beer on the floor

by the bed, but the burning
inside my heart was not
passion, but fear

and the beer smelled
and the sun was too bright
and I just wanted to be without

The Bad Dream

Jay Sizemore

Why not me?
Why not me?
Why not me?

I remember her screams,
and the sounds of belts lashing,
the light pouring out from under
the bathroom door,
the cold floor on my bare feet,
and the shadows.

Voices whispering through
gritted teeth and tears,
all incoherent now,
but the meaning remains.

It makes me scared.

I sneak back to my top bunk,
shiver beneath my Star Wars blankets
and childhood confusion,
the world growing darker.

The door opens
and he ushers her back
to the bottom bunk,
her bare feet
much smaller than mine.

He kisses her goodnight
while she is still crying,
the belt still clenched
in his callused left hand.

I remember his face
floating above his white t-shirt,
hair disheveled, lines creased
in his forehead,
black eyes in the night
that were blue in the day,

shaking with fury
and something I didn't understand,
maybe guilt.

He sees me.

I smell his cigarette breath
as he leans in to whisper,
"You want some too, boy?"

Staring into the eyes of a demon,
I can only shake my head
and listen to my sister's sobs
as he stalks away,
and it all starts to fade
like a bad dream.

Monster in My Closet

Patricia A. Hawkenson

A crack of light
is all I see
from where
I sit.

My feeling of safety
ever shrinking
smaller
so

I come to hide
away from
you
or

sitting in the laundry basket
fingers in my ears
shut the closet
door.

It holds out the sight
but not the sound
I fear from
you

making noises, shouting
bangs against
the floor.
STOP!

I'm afraid, and so I stay
hugging my jeans
wet against
my eyes

trembling fingers
clenching air
alone and
scared.

My mind is shouting
back at you,
"Leave her
be!"

Please, how can I stop you
hurting her with sounds
only echoing deep
in here?

I don't know what to do
so I'm huddling quietly
listening fingers
in my ears.

You know I'm small, don't you
see I haven't the strength
to keep out
the fear

that's growing in the closet
from frightening noises
unable to shut out
or see?

Lurching at me through the door
overtaking rationed reason,
I'm wiping at my
tears

that dripping down splash
upon my stomach,
tightly
ill.

Scraping scuffle of feet
and turning knob
door flies open -
FEAR!

Bright light shocking
eyes closed tight
do I dare look
up

at wild eyes searching
for a secret quiet
place to
hide?

Gasp of quickness
pulling
in now -
SHH!

Four ears listening
but not hearing
any little
sound

that comes in sneaking
in between the
hands upon
our ears.

Holding tight now,
somehow stronger,
two against
the fear.

4. SHOCK

As if someone has landed - A fist to my heart, I cry out - Oh no, oh no, oh no
S.E. Ingraham – R.S.V.P. to the Uninvited

A mere 8 years to laugh and to play - Now daisies will grow on her grave
Patricia Anne McGoldrick - Victoria

Darkness Provides

Laura Hegfield

gazing out the window into
black
pierced by
distant clusters
of twinkling lights
huddled
discreet
not blazing
not glaring
respectful of the secret sacredness
darkness provides

our eyes adjust as we turn
away
now toward
intimacy
facing fears
frailty
searching for familiar
for known
safe within the sanctuary
darkness provides

so i ask you:
what is the blessing
harbored
in this mysterious
moonless
winter night?

and i tell you:
discovering that our own
holy
interior light
has been beaming all along
in this body
this refuge

YES
darkness provides

Innocence Destroyed
Barbara Ehrentreu

She wears her innocence
like a shield
Yet his sword rips into her
Uncaring of her baby soft skin
and unexplored regions
It slashes beyond the barrier
turning bubblegum dreams
into nightmares
as she hears him say,
"Daddy wouldn't hurt you."
But it's too late
she has locked herself
in a secret place and
swallowed the key

RSVP to the Uninvited

S.E. Ingraham

She asks me if I remember you
And of course I do but still
We dig out the pictures from
Kindergarten on and there
Your awkward self smiles shyly

From the back row centre
Eyes roundly hopeful in your
Too-thin face you stare
Past the photographer; do you
See the future already, I wonder

Two tours in Afghanistan
She says, before you came home
And hung yourself in your Mom's
Basement; I search your face
In each year's class photo

Try to remember how you were
At birthday parties -"Maniacally
happy," she reminds me - you hardly
ever got invited to anything -
"Except that damned war," she says
"He felt invited to that."

"No!" I exclaim. "He must have
wanted to go or he wouldn't
have gone back... "
She shakes her head; no doubt
at my gullibility, in this area,
of all things.

Bits and pieces of who you were
Float back to me for days ...
Frightened when the dog barked
Afraid to laugh out loud
Even when something funny happened

What makes some children so fragile
I remember pondering that back then
And find myself worrying over it again
Now after your death – staring at your
Photos, especially this one candid

I have a shot of you taken when you
Weren't aware of the camera
You are standing off to one side
At a party at our place and the look
On your face breaks my heart

You look bewildered, a lost child
Of maybe six years old, you look,
With your shoulders rounded, chest
Caved in, haunted eyes – as if you
Have no idea where you are

Or worse, how you got there or why
Your mouth is partially open
But not in awe or as if you're about
To smile, no – there is a look
Of such despair in your face

I wonder at having missed this
The first time I went through these
Pictures – I sigh and go to put them
Away – notice I have penciled something
On the back of that most disturbing one

It's your name and NB, (the Latin
abbreviation for notation ...)
To myself, I have made the note –
"Try to find out what's wrong here ...?"

Then, life must have got in the way
And I put you away with the rest
Of the pictures and put you
Out of my mind ...

As if someone has landed
A fist to my heart, I cry out
Oh no, oh no, oh no
How could I be so careless
With your sad little life, I wonder

I know how irrational I am being
I know that no one can be everywhere
At once, be all things to everyone
But right at this moment, I feel
So utterly inadequate, so much
Not the person you needed me to be

As I turn that photo over and over
Trying to remember why I took it
In the first place – why photograph
A child's misery if you weren't going
To try and help the child?

My child has come back into the room
Sees me with the photograph
Takes it and says —
"Oh Mom - you're not beating
yourself up about this are you?"

It must be all over my face
As she gently reminds me
How I couldn't save the world
Not now, not back then ...
Not ever ...

Waiting
Jane Penland Hoover

Against thick walls
white-brick,
wisteria blooms, a purple wash
suspended

those hemmed in within
separated
from what was their life.

When does one learn,
accept the world
will not return to the colorful
splash of once upon a time?

She screams

Pearl Ketover Prilik

At the top of the stairs
in footed Wonder-Woman pajamas
tousle-haired unbraceleted
awakened toddler girl

Wide eyed watching
Crayon red rage rising in
Daddy's face
His ever to-her-gentle hand
Slapping, smacking
Fisting
Mommy's quiet
crumpled head

Heart thudding with his beat time
Drumming fast in tiny neck
At the top of the stairs
She stands
In silent impotence

Watching
in footed Wonder-Woman pajamas

Until with super-sonic
shatter warning pierce
Splintering, breaking, racing,
Stretching beyond

She screams
Through time

The Fairy Tale Ending

Diana Terrill Clark

The world swims before me
I feel gravity shift
for a moment
and I wonder crazily
what my expression
must be.

Everything is changed.
Every conception I had
about us
about our life
about love and
working
things
out
is all gone
is all changed
and somehow
my innocent love
has become a
horrible
mockery.

Did I really hear you say it?
You don't love me.
You feel, somehow,
you never have
loved me.
And me sitting
on the couch
with my world rocking
like a tipsy
rowboat.
Everything
that has been said
between us,
everything
that has been done
between us
is somehow rotten,

reeking,
redolent of shame
and this
horrifying feeling
that I somehow
should have known
about the women,
about your true feelings
washes over me
like a tsunami
inevitable
and filled
with the debris
of my world.

And I consider
our fairy tale romance
and realize
the Grimm brothers
didn't always write
happy endings
either.

Victoria
Patricia Anne McGoldrick

What a regal name
For such a small girl
Not more than a princess so young
A mere 8 years to laugh and to play
Now daisies will grow on her grave
All the long day.

Dedicated to the memory of Victoria (Tori) Stafford, July 15 2000-April 8 2009.

5. DEPRESSION

fists plunged into the suds, lips like chalk, - holding back the scream when her thumb - thrusts into the soaking bread knife.
J.lynn Sheridan – No more singing

I fell into a slimy pit - Slippery slopes kept me in - Friends shouted from sunlit skies - Their ropes only reached half way
Connie L. Peters – The Slimy Pit

No more singing

J.lynn Sheridan

Steam haloes her head,
nibbling at the fringes of her ashen hair,
puckering the flaps of skin around her neck,
the sigh in her eyes, flaccid from ache.

Dove soap lathers up her forearm,
sliding, cascading over the fork in her
hand to her black-nailed toes on the
linoleum, a weak power stance at the sink.

She is scouring the sky for red hawks.

One raw voice plucked from behind pizza
sauce caked in his beard with a serpent
cough says, "How come you don't sing
when you wash dishes no more?"

Her eyes are chained to a soaring hawk,

fists plunged into the suds, lips like chalk,
holding back the scream when her thumb
thrusts into the soaking bread knife.

A Woman Stretched Too Thin

Meena Rose

Helpless and Worthless;
Sad and Dejected;
Angry;
Raging and Incensed;
Fearful and Terrorized;
Frightened;
Cowering and Grieving.

The words repeat.
The sensations repeat.
She has learned to see them repeat.
She acquiesces quietly to the vicious dance;
That shreds my soul with each step.

Who am I? What am I? Why am I?
Is her refrain.
Life's greatest quandary.
Is there truly someone trapped within?
Am I myself's comatose dream?
Is my soul trapped in a foreign body?
Again... What am I?

The rage unending;
Waves crashing and unrelenting;
Destruction and Bleakness;
Arid;
Alone and Wandering;
Seeking and Searching;
Grasping;
Desiring and Lusting;
Nothing and Stillness Unending;
Whimpering;
Crying and Raging;
Finally Collapsing.

Waking and Acknowledging;
Hiding and Failing;
Accusing;
Rejecting and Denying.

Mercifully, the day goes on;
Then the night comes;
The darkness and the quiet;
Reflection.

The Crystal Chalice is cracking;
The Crystal Chalice is breaking;
The Chalice has broken;
The Blood finally runs free.

Deep in the House

Patricia A. Hawkenson

My curtains are drawn shut.

I have condemned myself
to endless puttering
dusting my brick-a-brac,
the miscellaneous objects,
furniture and curios
I raked up over the years.

Till coffee brews
to dispel my fog
allowing me to finally see
where what I value
has been shit upon.

So I scrub it all
within an inch of its life
for it is all I have
and if God is willing,
it will shine again.

But God help me,
for my arms are tired.

Sort of Blue

Jane Shlensky

Sort of Blue
She wants me not to notice,
And so she takes my hand
And smiles that old apology and says,

Do you ever have days when you feel
Sort of blue for no reason?
Just crucified by everything and nothing?

Days when you wonder what the point of living is
And nothing seems to be worthy of any sort of Maker?
Do you look at yourself sometimes and see

emptiness and think of your passing
As the absence of nothing? Hearing the news—
Wars and cruelty and corruption—

Do you feel ashamed of being human?
And seeing the beauty of the world,
The birds and flowers and wonders here,

Do you feel ashamed of being ashamed?
Maybe it's me, but do you ever feel this way?

Her kind suffering eyes look into mine, so like
Her own, awaiting my answer mirrored there:

Yes. All the time. I am my mother's daughter.

Insomnia

Jane Penland Hoover

Three a.m. ~awake again~
eyes wide with dread
cold complicated silence
bosom clutch of possible.

Double mind of angled arguments
flung again and again at walls
silent against all threat.

Days lost to turning through
 guilt married to disturbance
 birthed moments unwanted
 jagged grief refusing our dismissal
as lungs demand breath after breath.

Awake and awake, still
I watch snow sift
its layered shroud
 imagine slipping under.

Mourning Chill

S.E. Ingraham

Chill she was the bitter breeze of mourning who casually
Lay claim to my unsuspecting soul, so simplistic in nature
Both soul and breeze conspired to obstruct the slightest breath
Or beat of heart, or pulse, or firing of any of brain's lonely synapses
As they stood sentient, or so they felt themselves to be
But were, alas, imposters even unto each other, never sensing
Their rot had long begun in early times and cell-regeneration
Was merely theory, like global warming or world peace
Unproved, untried, and certainly unlikely
Cobwebs of confusion knit together with half-remembered thoughts
Until a melange of such terrible beauty has me wishing
For some order, some relief – even if that means, the blackness of
The blankness of – oblivion – the unknowing void just there
And then just beyond –surely there be restful release at last

Sad Song in February

Marian J. Veverka

Outside the restaurant the sidewalk is swept bare
Only a thin band of dirty snow
Traces the cracks and breaks
And a few dark sparrows
Huddled down into their feathers
Hop about old papers and dead leaves.
The pale, washed-out sun
Tries to pick its way through the grimy windows
And I pick at my breakfast
That's congealed on my plate
Like a moment that's gone on too long.
My coffee is as bitter and dark
As tears held back long after
The time to cry has passed.
Now, as I watch, the sun gives up
To a few mangy clouds which pause
Long enough to spit
Some spiteful flakes of snow.
I dab at crumbs with my napkin and think of you
In this dull place where even sunlight
Gives up trying to enter...
In this drained out end of winter
Which has dragged itself out over
The buildings and the streets
Until all the sounds are muted by cold
And the colors dulled by snow.
I could leave now and go back
To where the empty, unmade bed
Gapes in the middle of our apartment
Like a mouth caught in a frozen howl
And the empty dresser drawers
Drop open in amazement.

Where the silence screams over and over
Drowning out the stereo and TV
Until that great fist of your absence
Hurls me back into the streets
Where I huddle with the hungry sparrows
Eternally waiting for the crumbs of your presence.

The Slimy Pit

Connie L. Peters

I fell into a slimy pit
Slippery slopes kept me in
Friends shouted from sunlit skies
Their ropes only reached half way

Slippery slopes kept me in
I felt all alone
Their ropes only reached half way
Darkness engulfed me

I felt all alone
Weighed down in sorrow
Darkness engulfed me
I heard a Voice

Weighed down in sorrow
Isolated from friends
I heard a Voice
A light shone in the darkness

Isolated from friends
One Friend remained
A light shone in the darkness
He showed me the toeholds

One Friend remained
He smiled at me
He showed me the toeholds
We climbed out together

He smiled at me
We held hands
We climbed out together
One fell in, but two came out

We hold hands
Shouting in sunlit skies
One fell in, but two came out
Of the slimy pit

Your Photo Remains

Pamela Smyk Cleary

I keep trying to write, but
sometimes, in uninspired moments
my mind meanders, my eyes
wander the room, seeking out
your photographs
collaged upon the wall

I hear your laughter,
can feel you
creeping up behind,
distracting wisp
your breath across my neck,
smile pressed to my shoulder,
luring me away
from work, due dates,
assignments

Only an illusion, I know,
trick of the mind
and heart;
all that remains
are your photographs,
my deadlines
and
I keep
trying to write,
but

Voices

Richard Walker

Boy is sent to his room
without dinner or explanation
"You should know why"
(the voice of passive aggression)

Boy is hurt
but has no outlet
for that emotion
(the voice of anger is also wrong)

So he dampens the flame
says he feels nothing
because that's better than pain
(the voice of thought over emotion)

The boy is blue
the world a sadder place
though no one notices
(the voice of depression grows stronger)

He's a sensitive boy
He's so shy
You know how introverts are
(the voice of rationalization)

So no one sees his pain
he hides it even from himself
but it grows within him
(waiting for the voice of compassion)

Eulogy For A Teenage Daughter

Patricia Anne McGoldrick

Through his tear-filled eulogy
The anguished Father said—

She

had taken to wearing a t-shirt,

you know,

the kind that teenagers wear,

with a saying

I've   got   issues

When it should have been reading

**HELP ME,
MOM AND DAD!**

Note: Poem on this sad occasion is used with the permission of the late girl's father.

6. EMPOWERMENT

She wrote that day, "I don't need - to learn another thing in my life.-
I need to survive what I know.
Jane Shlensky – Born Old

his relentless search to uncover - the truth for other fathers
Barbara Ehrentreu – Semper Fi

Ways to Grapple With Ghosts

Meena Rose

You find yourself jerked awake;
Adrenalin coursing through your veins;
You try to run away and you can't;
Something is holding you down;
You strain harder as his sneer becomes louder.
Then you open your eyes and
Realize that it was only a shade of
Your rapist come to pay his respects.
You promptly collapse in the bed
As you send up a prayer
Asking for protection.

You find yourself crying inconsolably;
Under the benevolent warming sun.
Your friends turn around and look at you
As your feet take flight;
Tears streaming down your cheeks.
When you stop running
You realize that it was only a shade of
The man you witnessed die.
You promptly take a deep breath
And send up a prayer
Asking for comfort.

You find yourself sad and thirsty
While all those around are happy;
Drinking from Nature's cup to intoxication.
You see Life before you and can't engage;
You are stuck in the shaded vale
Held captive by the Ghosts of Death and Violence
Who seek you out relentlessly should you step into Life
To which your only defense
Is faith and hope
Which in turn
Imbue your
Spirit with
Resilience

Born Old

Jane Shlensky

"I want to know if I can live with what I know, and only that." Albert Camus

That girl was old at fourteen,
her hair all split ends and fury,
her eyes outlined with kohl
that exaggerated her world weariness,
her eyes receding into the palest
painful painted face.

At the group home where she lived,
she parented the small children,
befriended the older girls, a nurturer.
In my class, she penned pleading letters
to her relatives during writing time,
then tore them slowly into strips.

She told a boy complaining of his mother
that he was too stupid to live, but before
I could call her to account, she began to cry
and said if she could live with her mother,
she'd kiss the woman's feet every day.

A huge shy boy reached out his hand
and touched her shoulder and said he knew
just how that was. No one spoke much after that.
Instead, we wrote about what was in our broken
hearts, about how life can come knotted and torn to us,

how our own people can betray the very love
we bear them, and strangers can lift us up,
about good dogs and bad luck and how
it might be possible to live on our own terms.
We wrote and learned our own lessons that day.

At close of class, I watched them leave tamed
by witnessing wounds and watching the weave
of kindness and need, knowing it began
with her hard face, still unhealed
by writing or schooling or friends.

She wrote that day, "I don't need
to learn another thing in my life.
I need to survive what I know."
And she'd never heard of Albert Camus.

I Am Not Alone

Connie L. Peters

I am not alone
I'm not fatherless
I'm not forsaken
Nor unloved

I have a shoulder to cry on
Someone to rely on
Someone who accepts me as I am
And cares for me completely

I am not abandoned
Nor abused
I am not left out in a storm
Like some stray kitten

My needs are met
My joy is full
My hope is sound
My home's beyond the sky

In The Glow

Pearl Ketover Prilik

In the glow
of chaos swirling
from the brush of
butterfly wings
to cataclysm rises
from the confines of
ash behind barbed wired
smokestacks to the
lap of clear aqua waters
on a manicured fingertip
In the glow of chaos swirling
Each to the other connected
Through the tempest of time
Rising from each cindered soul
Floating from buildings terrible
Tumble into bottomless eyes of big bellied
Children's – sunsoaked run in suburban sprinklers

In summer eves that melt into
Arctic airless black
In the glow
From first outraged scream to last shuddered sigh
All that has been, is, and will be
From this besotted bare bone sharded
Unfamiliar landscape whirling in joyous
Confident abandon the constant
Shimmering configuration of a single slivered spark
In the glow

Hollow Spaces Hallowed Places

Laura Hegfield

often it is around the twists and curves
beneath the gnarled surface
within the hollow spaces
between the arch of bending
the act of turning
that life reminds us to wake up
to discover beauty in unexpected places

I will learn to stay rooted like an ancient tree
discover my own beauty in unexpected places

tired twisted gnarled body on the surface
hollow spaces revealing hallowed places
where soul and love and
creative life force swirl
expanding in spirals
I am at the edge of this vast inner wilderness
finding peace, in the act of writing these words

Being Super

Rosemary Nissen-Wade

I am not
the small, lone girl who
runs and jumps
on her lawn.
I am strong: beyond hurt. I
am power now. Me.

My cloak floats
out from my shoulders.
One leap and
I fly high,
up, up and AWA-A-A-A-Y — oh yes,
I am Superman!

Still, Passions, Still

Diana Terrill Clark
(after W.B. Yeats)

O Heart, be at peace because
Nothing more can be done
To cure a love with all its flaws,
To make two hearts be one,
Or return the remiss love;
It cannot be recovered.
Though you pray to gods above;
Though you wail; you beat, you flail;
Fresh passion you've discovered;
Poor heart, you cannot prevail.

Learn the calm and lasting peace,
Heart, they say will soon prevail
With time and luck, the pain will cease,
Be more mellow and more pale.
Right now this bitter-sweet relief
Is not what passion craves
It throws itself upon the rocks
It wants to rave, to storm!
In time, if my poor heart behaves
I know it can transform.

Semper Fi

Barbara Ehrentreu

His eyes fill with tears
flowing down the crags
of his face
the landscape of a broken
man who looked back to
the days when his precious
daughter held his hand and
romped in her nine year old
innocence in the grass as
they played

Those days were gone now
His beloved daughter wasted
from the leukemia she received
A present from the Marines
A present he now wishes to
return and go back to that life
when she was healthy and whole

Instead he stands before strangers
reciting words he has memorized
and bathed in his tear-filled nights
spent poring over the documents
telling him they poisoned his daughter
with taken for granted water, and
he thinks of the
stone he must face instead of his little girl,
her wasted life
his relentless search to uncover
the truth for other fathers

*Based on the documentary "Semper Fi" which is an
examination of the events at Camp LeJeune and the
contamination of their water causing cancer, leukemia and
birth defects. This is the man whose daughter's name is on
the new bill still waiting to pass in Congress.*

Repression

Jay Sizemore

Memories like that never seem to go away,
even if you burn all the pictures,
even if you cut him out of the ones
you couldn't afford to let go
for fear of forgetting the good parts
of raising your third child.

He had nothing he could want to forget,
but in his mind, the absence of a past
he might prefer to erase was the problem.

It's hard to know who you are,
without an idea of who you could have been.

Twenty-two years later, and that idea was dead.

I felt the relief of years stacked against
a closed closet door slip through the cracks
in my basement floor so I could look inside it,
pull the chain that turns on the bare bulb,
and see that the monster was gone,
though his claw mark scars would always remain
where the beast had struggled for decades
to scratch its way free from its cage.

But that same door I could finally open,
was for him forever sealed shut,
closed up like a tomb with stones
too heavy to lift, buried by the weight
of the years of an entire life without a face
to attach to a feeling of emptiness,
a feeling of loss locked up inside him
like a well without a bottom.

So, we decided to visit the grave.

I don't know how you say good-bye
to someone you never knew,
I went to put my pain at the foot
of the headstone like a bouquet of black roses,
while I think he wanted to let go
of hating something he could not touch.

We rode with a cousin neither of us really knew,
in a truck crowded with squeaky noises
and reminders of childhood tragedies
around every bend in the road
like some kind of ambush
set by a ghost,

pictures in the frame of the windshield glass
haloed with the luminescence of memory
and a mixed bag of feelings,
like swallowing a thumb tack
coated in honey.

We walked to the marker
and read his name,
set in the finality of stone,
but somehow it still seemed fake.

The inscription asked a Lord
to take his hand,
but no god would have ever
allowed such a man to live.

There was silence, under a gray January sky,
a light mist of rain adding an extra chill
to the wind of late afternoon,
as we stood, smoking cigarettes,
not knowing what to say,
but feeling it anyway.

He says he feels like breaking something,
wishes he could dig him up,
just so he could shit in his casket,
but instead he takes one of the decorations,
a clear plastic guitar, and puts it in his pocket.

We start back to the truck cause it's getting late,
and I let them get ahead of me,
I spit on the grave, whisper "fuck you,"
feeling grateful for once that my brother
never got the chance to call you his father,
and I never got the chance to kill you.

Trail of Broken Glass

Michael Grove

When you look back
all you see there are the fragments.
All the broken little pieces scattered there...
and you're naked and you're bleeding
and you're needing to walk on
to the smoother glass ahead without a care.

There are mirror fragments laying there all face up.
There are broken stained glass pieces strewn about.
There are shattered window panes
which have sliced your feet to shreds.
There are broken bottles that you laughed about.

Move ahead the glass is still so smooth and perfect.
No bearing weight to crack or chip the face.
The windows over stained glass over mirrors,
give you strength and beauty, dignity and grace.

When you look back
all you see there are the fragments.
All the broken little pieces scattered there...
Now you're naked and you're bleeding
and you're needing to walk on
to the smoother glass ahead without a care.

Café au Lait
Pamela Smyk Cleary

A secluded table in the corner
sports two lovely women --
huddled together,
sipping, smiling, laughing.
On the surface they've got
nothing in common --
pale peaches 'n' cream
mingling with café mocha.
Some might assume them lovers
maybe, but they'd be wrong.

Sweet tea magnolia and
blackstrap molasses --
to all appearances,
the best of friends --
sharing their sisterhood,
collaborating in a common goal.
Recognizing the black barracuda
as a barrister, you might
perceive a business partnership
but you'd only be partly right.

Fettered instead by family ties,
combining the hard-headed business sense
they inherited from a common ancestor,
they're selling off his stables, dismantling his
mansion to finance a new wing for the
Harriet S. Tubman Children's Hospital.

Planning to name it after him, they laugh
together over the possibility that,
just maybe, their great-great-grandfather
is rolling over in his grave.

Start: a definition
Daniel Ari

How audacious to call anything a start.
Start is a moment that's put on
auspicious clothing, a change in tempo
or intensity, but beneath that
just another continuation.

Start is the celebrity on the front page
of today's media section who was yesterday
somebody's neighbor, a person at the store
or walking through the parking lot,
like all of the rest of us.

Start is really only continue.
The infant's emergence only advances its gestation
from proteins incorporated
two or ten or a thousand generations past.
The New Year comes with a bang,
a pop and a dropping ball,
and then it's time for bed
because tomorrow we have to go on,
figuring this out. Start is
a thin party thrown by Continue,
sublimating quickly
as a champagne bubble.

7. CALM

just breathe - on your next - inhalation - the world - will change
Laura Hegfield – Just Breathe

Time of smooth routines, - us rising as light calls.

Walks around the pond ~ soft steps through the meadow
Jane Penland Hoover – Beyond Darker Years

We carried on, not thinking too much and - The seasons changed,
Marian Veverka - So We Decided to Keep on Waking
Up Every Morning

Just Breathe
Laura Hegfield

just breathe
on your next
inhalation
the world
will change
as you
exahale
you will
change
and all
is as
it needs to
be

opening
bright
foggy & dark
shifting
muted & quiet
expansive
nearer
oh so near
here
breathe
in
gratitude
exhale

He's in the ground and I am not

Jay Sizemore

Because he's in the ground and I am not,
I should see the beauty this life can bring,
and put those thoughts in the earth to rot.

The dead stay with us like cold blood clots,
their memory comes like winter's cruel sting,
but still, he's in the ground and I am not.

The things he did to us might still haunt
my thoughts like scars and wake me from dreams,
but I've put those thoughts in the earth to rot.

Time has changed me, but I've not forgot
the broken mirrors, the knives, the nightly screams,
but still, he's in the ground and I am not.

He forged my anger with the words he taught
through hot fists of fear his demons would sing
but I've put those thoughts in the earth to rot.

The devil inside him would have fought
to turn me against myself, to make my heart mean,
but since he's in the ground and I am not,
I've placed those thoughts in the earth to rot.

Ode to Five Calm Minutes

Patricia A. Hawkenson

You are becoming a slippery fish
sliding in and out of my frantic day
but when you and I can find each other
ecstasy ensues,
for I love you so.

There is no soul filling breath so welcome,
no back of my eyelids scenes so savored,
no dropping shoulders or kicking of shoes
that frees me,
that revives me,
that loves me
as much as my grasp on you,
five minutes.

Heaven is found
in our moments together!

Doldrums
Connie L. Peters

The sky is bluer than it ought to be.
Though February, the sun shines brightly.
The air is fresh and spring-like, but no wind.
I walk, clearing my mind as autos pass.

The call has gone out early this new year,
the yearning to go beyond the mundane—
my life I somehow unwittingly made.
The sky is bluer than it ought to be.

I deal with my stuff and the world still spins.
Each day the sun rises and life goes on.
I feel dull, alone, insignificant.
Though February, the sun shines brightly.

I'm grateful I don't have major problems.
I drift along on an untroubled sea,
no turbulent stressors rocking my boat.
The air is fresh and spring-like, but no wind.

I must learn to have patience with doldrums,
keeping steady, knowing wind will pick up,
when I'll sail along adventurously.
I walk, clearing my mind as autos pass.

Beyond Darker Years

Jane Penland Hoover

Time of smooth routines,
us rising as light calls.

Walks around the pond~
soft steps through the meadow

listening for blue birds,
spying the cardinal pair.

Time enough for us
another breakfast, lunch

then dinner. Later
turning in plush comfort

as darkness hushes birds.
Seven days sufficient

measure ~ for at last,
in-sync our dual breath.

August Apples for J.

Patricia Anne McGoldrick

Apples red
By the basketful he picks them
From that tree with the shiny green leaves over there
He picks them carefully
Like eggs from the nest of a prize laying hen
He places them
One by one
In the brown wooden basket

Then he lays out that old picnic blanket on the lawn
Sets up his apple-peeler
The one that he brought with them from Australia
Then he sits there
Lined up between the basket and the peeler and
He begins to peel those apples
Every August 11
He churns that peeler as his mind whirls round
With memories of his daughter
You see, he told me,
She would have been seventeen today
She could have been packing for university
If…But…

J's Dad is peeling apples today
Peeling round and round and round and round
Just adds cinnamon, he does
Apples have a natural sweetness, he says.
J's Dad is peeling apples today
Round and round and round and round and…
You see,
J's birthday was today….

In memory of J. who was born August 11 1988 and died October 7 2005.

Our Quiet House

Pearl Ketover Prilik

Mother had long hair
Fell to her waist
As it swept my cheek

When I hugged her
After preschool

Once I saw my father
Brush her hair hard in
Long strokes on their bed

Another time I saw
My father wind her
Hair around his wrist

And pull her to the kitchen floor
Kicked her baby belly
No baby waiting anymore

My mother cut her hair
He left forever

I don't remember which
came first

I know she
sprayed rose mist in the air
and softly, softly brushed
her short shimmery hair
in the slanted sunlight

of our quiet house

I Start My Evening Walks

Rosemary Nissen-Wade

I start my evening walks again
after a long gap,
plodding tired and heavy
at the end of the day
in a still chilly dusk.

Head down, I'm surprised
by clover dotting the grass,
little happy faces.
A lone ibis flies,
stretching in a straight line
for the hills of home.

Only ten minutes today.
I turn about
and the round moon confronts me
low in the sky, bright white.
Now I am peaceful.

So We Decided to Keep on Waking Up Every Morning

Marian J. Veverka

And when I plugged in the coffee
I never paused to ask "why" just
Did it, put your Cream of Wheat
In the microwave while I watched
The Weather Channel. Which never
Lets you down. Every day, there's
Always weather. And we can talk about
It if the silence gets too heavy. And it
Is better than the news because there was
A war going on at the time and it seemed
Like all our lives we were either in one or
Between one or a cold one and so much
Trouble in the world and what was our
Loss compared to so many, so many lives?

We carried on, not thinking too much and
The seasons changed, winter arrived so
We stayed in the house a lot and I was able
To read books again and we could watch
TV and sometimes laugh at some dumb
Thing and look at ourselves, surprised.

Hidden Inside Me

Barbara Ehrentreu

People see the calm and quiet
demure together woman
speaking in a low voice
sitting calmly in Starbucks,
vanilla skim latte in hand
they don't know the
burning fire inside, the
anger waiting,
sparked in private, peeking only
rarely, when it can no longer
be tamed, flaming in public
The fire voice strong and firm
taking no prisoners retreating
from no one
demanding to be heard at the
smoking of slightest injustice
yet, usually, it stays hidden within
only appearing when safe
in the confines of my home
where the lion no longer
need be caged.

8. TRUST

Put out your hand - like a branch breathes buds - in the spring.
Ina Roy-Faderman – Reach like a tree

If you are interested - in beating the odds, - embrace them.
Daniel Ari- Accept Except

Chances

Jane Shlensky

Some days my memories with you fog,
and I cannot imagine your voice
or mine, as we were when you were
most yourself. Still, my hands are yours,
worn and busy, stained with foliage,
and my hair, white long before its time,
traces a gene back to your mother.

I carry you in me, as I concentrate
on opening earth to seedlings,
trying to sense seasons' change,
smelling soil and new buds,
spring rains and twilight,
checking old growth bark for new life—
all learned from you.

I gather words together, arranging them
like posies, pruning and shaping
just as you taught me,
a poem helping us share a moment
of observance, a recognition
of overlooked wonders in need
of second chances: the first crocus,

a jay's feather, a gnarled twig like a cross,
a stone laced with red veins pulsing
the heart of the earth,
a dead hummingbird
curled like a small fist,
lying still
among wild flowers.

I know when you became uprooted
from yourself, you longed for death,
but I could not wish you gone,
even knowing all I'd learned
of pain and loss, that death is not
the worst thing, still I could not imagine
a world depleted of you.

I cannot now say "never" in a line
that has you in it. You are ever.
As long as I can remember,
I will feel you living in me
and take every spring's resurrection
as a chance to hold you again.

Letting Go
Connie L. Peters

It sounds so simple.
Open your hand.
Let things fall where they may.

In reality,
it can be
like sawing off an arm or leg

Deep pain
Determination
Learning to do without

Sometimes letting go means
grabbing on to something else.

Walking Alone
Marian J. Veverka

This sunshine warm against my face
Will not touch yours. Nor will I see
Your cheeks flush rosy in the wind,
Your head bowed against the rough
Tumbling of advancing Spring.
How you welcomed the lengthening
Daylight, the twilight star poised above
The neighbor's barn, the willow tree
Veiled in palest green and the wild forsythia
Carelessly spilling gold across the neighborhood.

These things I see.
Alone on the empty afternoon
Sidewalk, looking down, avoiding what
I cannot share—how long the road, how sad
The solitary journey. Haunted by memory
That comforts as it wounds. Still let it be
My shadowy companion.

Ten hundred
Thousand days and nights are not infinity
Listen to the Redwing's song, the Sparrow's patter,
The hum and bustle of the days, a smile for me.
Awaken, all my senses, I pass this way but once.
Let every step I follow lead me home to you..

From Earth: A few questions

So how much do the dead know
About what is going on in the
Land of the living?
Is it true that their spirits, invisible,
Pass in and out among us?
It has always been my hope that
My mother, who died when I was
In my teens
Might be able to see and know
My children.

When my daughter passed from this life
Did the grandmother she never knew
Appear beside her and
Take her hand?

Coming Out of the Dark

Rob Halpin

Her light long ago tamped
leaving her a shadow
of her former self
living in the shadows
of her former world

His light tentatively intrudes,
scattering her shadows,
the black and gray of her world,
threatening exposure of colors
long hidden in her sanctum

She's coaxed into his light,
laying bare her fears, her pain,
stark and unhidden, still raw,
trusting in his promise
of enduring light and hope

In the Shadow of Stroke…
the Aftermath of Aphasia

Jane Penland Hoover

More than a list of nouns,
language transfers meaning
from one heart to another,
informing, questioning,
encouraging.

Last week
at our four-party dinner table
our friend said, "We ate
at the best Thai restaurant
at Main and Greene."

"I know the spot! Next door
is a barbecue shack
I can't name…
Sometimes our daughter
Rhonda meets us there."

Then he uttered
his single words,
added gestures.

Name…SameThing…Ugh…
Charleston…Holly…Jim…Ahw…
Aw…SameThing…Four…More.

When he tries to speak
I no longer want to guess.
Thirty-four years since that stroke,
yet again, I am trying to
fit together the puzzle
of his thought.

Aha, I've got it! Sticky Fingers,
the barbecue place in Charleston
where we ate three years ago
with our other daughter Holly,
her husband Jim.

I say, "Sticky Fingers".
Ron pushes his notepad toward me.
I write "Sticky Fingers."
He smiles.

In his aphasia group
on Monday, he may say:
Charleston...Holly...EatIt...
Ahw...Longtime...ThisOne...
SameThing...uh...eat...

Then press his fingers together,
hold as if they will not come apart,
hoping they will say Sticky Fingers...
Maybe not.

For one small second
I imagined
he would tell our friends tonight
about another time and place

when he and I shared a table,
candlelight and music witnessing
our soft voices and bright eyes,
focused solely on each other.

Tonight he pockets pad and pen
then scans the room,
flashing his cheery smile
to all who look his way.
I feel alone, together.

He lifts his glass,
sips tonight's sweet tea.
I paint a smile across my face
straining to remember
to be grateful
for our efforts.

I Spoke to the Mirror

Michael Grove

I spoke to the mirror
and the mirror told me,
"You are who you are
and not what I see.

I can't see you inside
from this place on the wall.
With a heart that is golden,
you've got it all."

The mirror said, "Listen
I'll tell you the truth.
You haven't changed much
since you were a youth.

Your facade may be grayer
your wrinkles more bold.
With a heart that's so open,
you'll never grow old.

A reflection of you
is drawn here on my glass.
Don't worry at all.
This too shall pass."

Accept Except
Daniel Ari

Even one plus one
can surprise you
yielding a some-
thing that's true that's not two.

If you're certain,
run against your grain.
Closed curtains
are full of pinholes;
the bricks of the world
have hollow backs.
Chance tearing
the fabric.

If you are interested
in beating the odds,
embrace them.
To be specific:
nothing's odd
that's held close,
and nothing's true
that isn't false.

Where you're stuck,
take leave, and what
you can't believe in, believe.

Reach like a tree

ina Roy-Faderman

Put our your hand
like a shoot hoping
for a sunbeam.
Put out your hand
like a branch breathes buds
in the spring.
Put out your hand
like the tree reaches
for the clear sky.
Put out your hand,
and you need not say,
"I love you."
For your hand
can hold my hand,
and my hand can hold
the world's love.
Reach like a tree
Put out your hand
like a shoot hoping
for a sunbeam.
Put out your hand
like a branch breathes buds
in the spring.
Put out your hand
like the tree reaches
for the clear sky.
Put out your hand,
and you need not say,
"I love you."
For your hand
can hold my hand,
and my hand can hold
the world's love.

9. CONFIDENCE

learning to sing in the dark and I'm doing just fine.
J.lynn Sheridan - Whenever I think of you

Keeps reminding me how much - He loves me and says simply, "We will."
S.E. Ingraham – We Will

Whenever I think of you

J.lynn Sheridan

The night is empty without you and I'm
feeling a bit lost, wondering what you're doing
under this cold moon of time. There's a fine

line between a sad ending and a war, a fine
line between grief and death. Right now I'm
somewhere in between. Suffering is doing

the work in me that love couldn't—by not doing
for you, I've found a beauty in silence. I'm fine
with sitting in this space left by us. It's cold, but I'm

learning to sing in the dark and I'm doing just fine.

Ice Skater

Connie L. Peters

There seems to be a part of me
Afraid to relax and smile,
Afraid to say I'm okay
I'm God's beloved child.

Like a poor ice skater,
Shuffling on the rink
Cautious in each step
Caring what others think.

It seems I'm always wary
That I'll stumble and fall flat
And others will trip over me
Landing with a splat.

You want me to skate strong
Throw my head back in the wind
Smile and enjoy myself
As I glide along with friends.

Help me skate boldly
With a confident stride,
Knowing You are with me
Skating by my side.

Wounded by Words, New Hope Publishers (2008)

119

We Will

S.E. Ingraham

We're growing older, don't you know
—against the direst of predictions—
And even though there are still days
When I rail against the fates and think
I'll not be able to once again shrug off
the cloak of depression
There are many more days,
when I am now able to fight back
and kick open the drapes, defy the wrath
of this disorder, or that one ...

A year without a hospital stay in it
is a banner year - there has been
more than one in a row now ...
Isn't that something?
It is, believe me—
And, totally unexpected,
if you listen to the experts.
I know that a big part of the reason
I even exist is that man who's sleeping
on the couch over there pretending
to be watching the football game
While I'm over here with my laptop,
pretending to be a famous poet,
something he unabashedly encourages.

After more than four decades,
He's never given up on me, on us, not ever
Has not once thought about throwing in
the proverbial towel
Even when I was running amok
and spending the family savings
or doing even more outrageous,
unforgivable things -
All he ever really cared about was my physical
well-being, that I didn't hurt myself inadvertently
while my manias ran their course -
and they ran some pretty awful courses,
they did.

Whenever I fret or worry about
the future and, will we make it -
He always just hugs me, holds me tight
Keeps reminding me how much
He loves me and says simply, "We will."

Winter of the Past

ina Roy-Faderman

A seep of blue beneath
the metal window frame - slow, flowing river of
cold down the wall behind
my bed where I huddle
with my son's cold nose pressed
against my stomach under
the down duvet like a
blanket of snow and read
aloud mango poems of the Caribbean
to the silky crown of
his head so that while the
cold can swirl past our mouths,
it can never enter.

Three Years after his Stroke, the Day after Christmas

Jane Penland Hoover
(Aphasia: loss of speech with brain injury)

Together we stripped
tiny lights
repacked fragile balls and velvet bows~

his right arm hanging limp
his left hand grasping at the trunk~
We pulled
through aphasia's disarray. We
loaded one dry balsam
hauled it to the mall.

In that frozen season
few others came to
exchange one tree for another

from the volunteer,
who cleared her pile ~ gave us
ten root-thick dirt-bare sticks

to plant
in our hard yard~
where we watered, waited,

wondered at the audacity
of this labor.

Yet, today
birdsong lives
in ten leaf-full maples
lifting limbs into blue silence.

Always the Beckoning Beyond
Pearl Ketover Prilik

From stunned black and white confusion
on to pomegranate rage blossoming
in swirling profusion
glinting below ice fear-formed
shattered-safety, calm-exclusion

Always the beckoning Beyond

From the depths of forced depravity
To witnessed cruel war-ravaged inhumanity
From bloodied thighs, empty syringes, bottles broken
On lips of grim-faced doctors'
desks where vacant words staccato spoken

Always the beckoning Beyond

In the midst of chaos, fear and vomitous revulsion
Sweating, palpitating, mind racing,
just-too-hard-to-go-on vitality implosion

Always the beckoning Beyond

Moving, even while paralytic
Comfort when nothing is even vaguely analytic
Shining among buried bodies, limbs,
dreams, and trust, the whispered impetused *must*

Always the beckoning Beyond

Some soar and transcend past
where eye can see
Others breathe and empty minds of flotsam's
lingering debris
Some embrace, accept and befriend
Others sit in silken darkness and mend

All illuminated
bright filament-flickered steady spark
or flaring-roaring consuming conflagration
connected in the tapestried collective
of the shimmer-sparkling manifestation

Always the beckoning Beyond

Going After It

Diana Terrill Clark

"You only live once, but if you do it right, once is enough." —
Mae West

Life is short, it's very brief
I know this to my sorrow
I've known joy and I've known grief
and trouble enough to borrow.

Live your life, is my advice,
and live it to the fullest.
Procrastination has a price
even for the dullest.

Reach right out and grab your life
and seize the day with fervor.
Ignore the worries and the strife,
Don't be an observer.

Time is short and valuable
so treasure every moment
Yes, we all are fallible
but that just makes time potent.

The Apprentice

Meena Rose

I have been Chosen;
Chosen to learn;
Chosen to listen;
Chosen to remember.

Today is my Day;
Day to leave the old;
Day to start the new;
Day to marvel the future.

I have been Given;
Given to see without eyes;
Given to hear without ears;
Given to serve without hands.

Today is where I Begin;
Begin to draw emotion;
Begin to paint intent;
Begin to write hope.

Cease and Desist

Pamela Smyk Cleary

It's not as if you don't know
better. What could you be thinking?
You wouldn't treat your best friend
(acquaintance, perfect stranger)
so dirty, rotten, stinking.

Focused always on the flaws,
finding fault, name calling,
criticizing, griping, grousing,
bitching, caterwauling;

Have you nothing nice
to say? (Would I would listen
anyway?) Shut your trap!
Cease and desist!
Now you've got me really pissed!

You're nothing but a nasty sneerer.
Guess I'll try another mirror.

Until___

Barbara Ehrentreu

Until their words don't hurt me
my ears will pretend they can
bounce them like rubber balls
Fling words over the fence like
unwanted weeds

My feet will stay planted on the
ground I know and my body will be
a wall protecting the fragile underside
of my soul

Unaware of the barbs from
the scars of those fierce words
as they are pitched out willy nilly
Tearing the corners of
my clamoring ego

that tattered and pieced together
puts its brave face to the world
and ignores the mean spirits
as if they were feathers in the
air of my life.

10. LOVE/HAPPINESS/FULFILLMENT/PEACE OF MIND

Remind myself how strokes, -us taking turns -have brought us home
- to rest, side by side, -
> Jane Penland Hoover – Love Here

The twinkle of your eye speaks - Of hopes and dreams and climbing
peaks. Oh gentle spirit and tender heart, - Let me help play my part.
> Meena Rose – It Is Sleeping Time

A friend's story
J.lynn Sheridan

If you could just remain within your brick walls, insulate
yourself against the false ointment of Pharisees and thieves,
then these Roman cobblestones you tread upon
won't bruise your feet.

But, if isn't real and no one is that stubborn. So you strap on
your sandals and visit the prison where you kiss the son you
love under the radar of probing eyes, and
you scrub your mother's

floor as she scolds you, and you plug your ears to ranting bill
collectors and discontinue techie unnecessities,
and you sleep with extra blankets because
there isn't a body curved next to yours

any more. When that gets too heavy, I bathe your feet as you
have mine then we take out the china and spill our tears into
our chipped cups all the while recounting
the blessings that still remain within the walls of our friendship.

It Is Sleeping Time

By: Meena Rose

It is time to go to bed,
You are running away instead.
Come lay by me a while,
Let me see that endearing smile.

Beneath a canopy of stars,
Forgetting life's hurtful scars,
Two spots of light in the dark,
We take a walk in the celestial park.

Your hand in mine,
This is beginning to feel fine.
Feel my warmth as it flows to you,
You've been cold; feeling warm is overdue.

The twinkle of your eye speaks
Of hopes and dreams and climbing peaks.
Oh gentle spirit and tender heart,
Let me help play my part.

My Cristian, stay in my embrace
We are twin souls traveling in space.
It is now time for you to sleep,
This peace, I promise you I will keep.

Love Here

Jane Penland Hoover

Today is our forty-second anniversary
some years much longer than others
as time rolled us through, tumbled
us onto this now comfortable shore

Thick length of ills' dark heaviness
necessity upon necessity, rumbling
ruffling each hint of calm blue flow
in the waters of those days

Remembering I feel myself slipping
wanting to kick away, play
in the thick grass
of my father's once lush lawn

Where grass grew strong
despite the fact of his huge oak
spreading cool shelter in the melt-down
of Georgia's summer sun

Where Dad responded to neighbors
questioning his wisdom of children
playing there, and Day saying, We're
not growing grass but raising girls.

That red brick home, sweet corner
lives in my today's almost
more vibrant, vivid than then
at ten than now

When I no longer spin and spin
to let the craziness of dizziness
drop me into that green sea
but instead I reach up, lean close

Remind myself how strokes, one
and then another, us taking turns
to breathe, have brought us home
to rest, side by side, love here.

Growing Old Disgracefully
Rosemary Nissen-Wade

'A nude woman!'
he shouts with joy,
encountering me moving
thus unencumbered
from bedroom to bath,
bathroom to bed.

'Aren't you lucky!' I say.
'How many men of 82
have nude women
wandering their homes?'
'Not too many,' he guesses,
and grins. 'Yes, I am lucky.'

And I think to myself,
How many women of 71
have their nudity greeted
by men shouting for joy?
Not too many, I think.
I know who's lucky.

Turn around and around

ina Roy-Faderman

Outside child, you spin,
like a maple seed, earthbound, giggling as you fall.

Rising

Jane Shlensky

A juvenile hawk sits in the oak
near the pasture fence, calling repeatedly
to his own kind, plaintive in his loneliness.

His shrill keening echoes in me,
feathering the edges of my own closeted
otherness, my own failures and sorrows,

as I go about my day, displacing
him as the voice of my ennui,
until I hear his glad shriek aloft,

and look up into the morning light
to watch him riding the air currents,
circling, dipping, gliding,

befriending the wind,
offering succor, inspiring love,
my heart lifted on his wings.

Never Too Busy

Michael Grove

Never too busy to say I love you,
or reach out with an open hand.
Never too busy to rise above,
or to take a righteous stand.

I'm not talking self-righteous
if that is what you heard.
I'm talking about doing the right thing,
and speaking a peaceful word.

I'm talking about loving everyone,
every single day.
I'm saying don't harbor resentments
or live to make someone pay.

Never too busy to hear the word
amidst the mindless chatter.
Forgiveness and love are the answers.
The questions don't even matter.

This Gold Band
Pamela Smyk Cleary

This gold band,
no longer fitting my finger,
still encircles my life
encompassing the we
of you and me.

Constant confirmation.
Continuum of promises kept,
future intentions.

Engraved within,
your enduring message,
'Always'

The Fragrance of Love Exchanged
Laura Hegfield

joy in a most delicate form
a single fuchsia blossom
plucked from a crabapple tree
by the generous slender fingers
of a fourteen year old girl
on her way home from school

because it was beautiful
because she is kind

the dog barks
excited for the return of her friend
footfalls are heard on the stairs
then a soft knock on the frame
around the open bedroom door
she enters and sits on the rocker

for a moment
for a breath

turns her head to the right displaying her treasure
centers her face again
eyes alight and smiling
reaching up she eases the small gift from behind her ear
where she'd tucked it with care
so as not to crush it in warm hands

because it is fragile
because she is compassionate

graceful movements
the slightest vibration of pleasure
gently oh so gently
she places it in her mother's palm
both inhaling the fragrance
of love exchanged

he shouldered causes
Richard Walker

he shouldered causes
the ones that were broken
or which someone had dropped

he would bolt through the door
burst onto the scene
never asking to be forgiven

he would pull nonprofits from their shallows
jump through red tape hoops
as if he were dancing

his feet constantly moving forward
then gathered together to leap
over whatever hurdles there were

toppling indifference only
he was a burst of joy
striking like a bolt of love

On the road to awakening

Pearl Ketover Prilik

Wake to the sense of self,
count the numbers
of your years – shake the shock –
manage the melancholy
turn in the softness of
a feathered bed

to the gentle winding road
to the cool place within
scented with something

frangipangi,
an incense tree,
something spicy and sweet as
soft greenery drips draping
in splendid scented spill
over cedar shack sides
shining in shafted sun filigree

comfort in deep breaths
cool water poured on burning parts
deep breaths – unfolding tight parts
flow - loose -
ready -
now -

Open eyes and smile

Through the Portal

Rob Halpin

Lives eclipsed
blown through the portal
Dejected
And banished
Lost souls, shadows of themselves
groping in the dark

blinded by
their inner demons
disabused
and broken
cowering within themselves,
needing a beacon

lighting their
path, stoking their fires
defiant
and baptized
drawing on an inner strength
Climbing from the pit

full of hope
bursting from the mire
determined
and brazen
emerging from the portal
and moving beyond

POET BIOS

Daniel Ari holds an MFA in poetry and has self-published 12 chapbooks. His poems have appeared in Writer's Digest, McSweeneys, Turbulence, Pearl, Contact Quarterly, Chiron Review, Tattoo Highway, Jack Magazine, and many more print and online venues. He co-creates the poetry blog, IMUNURI (imunuri.blogspot.com) with Marna Cosmos. Daniel also presents solo performances based on poems he loves including ones by Cummings, Millay, Yeats, Roethke, Oliver, and Williams. He has presented segments of this work at The Marsh Theater in San Francisco and The Julia Morgan Theater in Berkeley as well as his home in Richmond. Daniel leads poetry and creative writing workshops at The Richmond Art Center (Richmond), Berkeley Tuolumne Family Camp (Yosemite), Improv Arts (Los Gatos) and at his home. In the last quarter century, in addition to writing poetry, Daniel has written novels; published film, food and book reviews; performed original music, theater, and stand-up comedy; and written marketing copy professionally for a huge range of companies.
Find more of Daniel Ari's writing at:
IMUNURI.blogspot.com
and
FightsWithPoems.blogspot.com.

Diana Terrill Clark is a legal secretary with multiple hobbies and a job she loves. She writes and has completed her first novel about a psychic detective whose encounters with bad guys of all description include a few with supernatural powers. She writes poetry, short stories, YA fiction, sews historical costumes, works on genealogy, cooks and bakes, knits, crochets, embroiders, and is in a band. She lives with her husband and two cats in Scottsdale, Arizona.
Drift of Bubbles: http://dianaterrill.wordpress.com

Pamela Smyk Cleary (a.k.a. PSC and 'PSC in CT') is wondering how she came to be included in this talented group of writers. Although she enjoyed writing poetry throughout her early years, she eventually graduated from college, got a real job, and fell into decades of poetic disuse. After almost 25 years as an Information Technology professional, she is currently in the process of rediscovering her "free time" and trying to balance all of her interests and commitments. In addition to dabbling in digital photography and attempting to recapture her elusive and recalcitrant muse, she also enjoys spending time with family & friends, hiking, biking, kayaking, bird watching and gardening. Despite her somewhat sporadic efforts, and the contrariness of said muse, some of her poems have actually been published – in Long River Run, Umbrella (online journal) and Every Day Poets (online); additionally, she has performed several poems before a live audience at Hi5netTV's "First Thursday" performances in Woodbury, CT. You may also, (if you are so inclined) find more of her poems on her (brand new & still being tinkered with) poetry blog "Wander, Ponder, Poems & Pics" @ http://wanponpopix.blogspot.com/

Barbara Ehrentreu is originally from Brooklyn, NY and she has lived in both upstate New York and the New York City Metro area. At the moment she lives in Stamford, CT with her family. She has a Masters in Reading and Writing K-12 from Manhattanville College. She started writing in third grade when her first poem was published in the School District Newsletter. She wrote poetry off and on for decades. However, only when she discovered Robert Brewer's Poetic Asides did she have her poem about the environment published. In addition to writing poetry she has written a children's story and an adult story both published online. Recently her young adult novel, If I Could Be Like Jennifer Taylor, published by MuseItUp Publishing won 2nd place in the Preditors & Editors Poll for Best Young Adult Book of 2011. She also has a story in the anthology, Lavender Dreams in memory of cancer victims, also published by MuseItUp Publishing. Furthermore, she has three poems in the anthology, Prompted: An International Collection of Poems published by Really Love Your Book, which was a collective effort by The Anthologists, edited by Pearl Ketover Prilik. While she is not writing or doing blog posts or interviews Barbara is a tutor for a private tutoring company.
Barbara's blog: http://barbaraehrentreu.blogspot.com/
Barbara's Facebook Author Page:
http://www.facebook.com/BarbaraEhrentreu
Find: If I Could Be Like Jennifer Taylor-
MuseItUpBookstore::http://tinyurl.com/6mp5guq
Amazon: http://tinyurl.com/6puspdb,
Nook: http://tinyurl.com/7cuuahu

ina Roy-Faderman was born in Lincoln, Nebraska to Bengali parents; most of her subsequent behavior has been an attempt to cope with this incongruity. She began her writing career at age 9 and went on to win numerous young writer awards, finally receiving formal creative writing training while completing an M.D. at Stanford University and a Ph.D. in Philosophy at U.C. Berkeley. Her fiction and poetry have appeared in such diverse venues as Highlights for Children, The Silver Web, Long Shot, India Currents and Pif Magazine. She lives near San Francisco with her spouse, a sprite, and a number of furry organisms, and teaches medical ethics and philosophy of science at Oregon State University.
http://Www.avromandina.net/ina

Michael Grove is a lifelong resident of Mid-Michigan. He is a writer and lyrical poet with a pure and simple style that comes from his heart and touches the soul. He has been writing hopeful and spiritually uplifting verse since he was 10 years old and dabbles at putting some of his poetry to music. He has published the first of a three-book series, "Observations: The 1st Four Dozen" and has completed "Observations: The 2nd Wave". He is putting the finishing touches on a faith-based poetry collection titled, "Reflected Light". His work experience includes college instructor, homebuilder, real estate broker and operations manager of a mortgage company. He enjoys all sports and is an avid Michigan State University and Detroit Tigers fan. Mike enjoys boating and fishing and appreciates spending quality time with his family and friends as well as his dog, Jake. He often says, "Learn from the past, Live in the Present and Look to the Future", and, "Pray for Peace, Hope for Joy, and Live for Love."
mikegrove7@yahoo.com

Rob Halpin is a soccer nut. He grew up an Army Brat and has lived in Hampton Roads, Virginia for the last 20 years. Rob began writing poetry a little over 15 years ago, has had a couple honorable mentions in poetry competitions, and has had one poem published prior to this anthology. Over the last year and a half, he has been active in the Poetic Asides blog on the Writer's Digest website. Aside from poetry, Rob has written a number of short stories (unpublished), aspires to write a novel, and tries to provide enough fresh content for his blogs for them to not get stale. All of this writing takes place (or doesn't) around a full time job in Information Technology, spending time with his wife and daughters, and playing, watching and coaching as much soccer as his wife will let him get away with.

Rob's blogs:

Wanna Get Published, Write!

(http://pubwrite.wordpress.com)

Lorwynd's Thoughts (http://lorwynd.wordpress.com)

Patricia A. Hawkenson is the author of 'Magnetic Repulsion, 100 Poems from Desire to Disgust.' It is available at:

http://outskirtspress.com/webpage.php?ISBN=9781432748 548.

Her poems and short stories have been published in numerous anthologies including: Prompted, An International Collection of Poems, Fandemonium Vol. 1 and 2, Four of a Kind, Royal Flush, and Clever Fiction. She is a National Board Certified Language Arts instructor in Eau Claire, WI and has won various awards for innovation and use of technology in education. Patricia enjoys many artistic expressions such as: stained glass, sewing tapestry handbags, and illustrating with watercolor pencils. Her poetry blog, Expressive Domain, contains hundreds of her poems. Enjoy them here:

http://www.phawkenson.edublogs.org./

Laura Hegfield is a daughter, sister, wife, mother and lover of life with an artist's soul, living on the edge of the woods in New Hampshire. Diagnosed with Multiple Sclerosis in 2009, she's no longer able to work outside her home as an art, yoga and meditation teacher due to disability. A strong believer in making lemonade from life's lemons and being of service through the abilities one does possess, she shares her journey candidly on her blog through photography, poetry, prose, essays and an occasional song. Laura also offers Spiritual Direction, Kaizen-Muse® Creativity Coaching and Lev b'Lev SoulCollage® facilitation on a limited basis, respecting her body's need for rest. In the winter of 2012, Laura opened The Healing Womb, a project of pure compassion. Her intention is to reach out to women, especially those living with chronic illness, who otherwise may not be able to attend meditation classes. She guides the group into meditation and silence for thirty minutes, sharing what she has learned about blessings held within life's inevitable challenges, creating community, one breath at a time. This is available to anyone in the world via a live tele-circle and free podcasts, honoring the reality that many individuals who are chronically ill are unable to work. Donations to support the effort and love she pours into The Healing Womb are gratefully accepted. Laura is a monthly contributor to Buddha Chick Life, a webzine "for women on the grow." She has also been a guest contributor at the On Being Blog, a public radio project, Carnival of MS Bloggers, and the Blog 4 a Cause E-book, to benefit cancer research. Beyond the Dark Room is the first "real" book in which Laura's work will be published.

Laura's website: www.shinethedivine.com

Laura's blog: http://www.shinthedivinecreativityisaspiritualpractice.com/

Jane Penland Hoover grew up in Decatur, GA, and graduated from Emory University in Atlanta, where she studied Business Administration and Accounting. She was the first woman hired as an Auditor by the US Department of Defense and worked for five years. Later, after her husband suffered a stroke resulting from surgery in 1973, Jane claimed a 25 year career with Clairmont Oaks, Inc., building and operating senior housing communities. In 1992 after her daughters graduated and married, Jane began facilitating creative writing groups and founded two writing guilds in Georgia before moving to NC with her husband in 2005. She continues to offer writing workshops, while writing memoir, poetry, developing her photography skills, enjoying grandchildren, sharing times with her mother and sisters. Jane has become a regular writer with online poetry groups like Poetic Asides and other Facebook groups, as well as posting to her own blog at http://jpenstroke.wordpress.com. Her poetry, memoir selections, and photography have been published in: Prompted An International Collection of Poems,The American Heart Association - Stroke Connect Magazine, Belladonna on line Magazine, Reflections: Dukes OLLI Memoir Collections, Oconee Cultural Arts Foundation Art Exhibits, Solstice Anthology Meredith College 2009, Portraits The Greensboro Writers Guild Volume XI 2009,

Reflections - The Greensboro Writers Guild Volume XIII 2011, Croasdaile Village Poetry Readings, Croasdaile Village Photography Exhibits,Croasdaile Village Voice
http://jpenstroke.wordpress.com

S.E. Ingraham lives and writes from the 53rd parallel: Edmonton, Alberta, Canada. She has always hoped it is the latitude at which she lives rather than her years as a mental health consumer that influences most of her work, but recently has come to accept that both factors may be equally at play. In any case, she has a manuscript in progress completely devoted to insanity ... Ingraham's work appears in several anthologies, among them: The Stroll of Poets (2009, 2010 and 2011), Rhythm International's, Sun and Snow (2010),the Raving Poets anthologies, Sofa King, Raving and 9 1/2, and Prompted - An International Collection of Poems (2011). She also has poems archived on poetsagainstwar.ca and at winningwriters.com, and has been published in the online u.k. 'zine melisma. New poetry from this writer may be found on her blogs:_THE WAY EYE SEE IT at http://aleapingelephant.blogspot.ca/
and THE POET TREEHOUSE at
http://thepoet-tree-house.blogspot.ca/

Patricia Anne McGoldrick is a Kitchener Ontario writer whose poetry and reviews have been published in the Christian Science Monitor, The WM Review Connection and, most recently, at ChapterandVerse.ca, a review of the award-winning, Plain Kate. Poems published recently include these titles: Neighbourhood Find, Spices of Childhood, Haiku on Winter at CommuterLit ; Girls and Green Apples in taking a bite of the apple--revelations anthology; Lockdowns in Verse Afire, volume 9, Issue 2, 2012. History, literature, the environment and upcycling resources for bookmaking are active interests, as well; often, the focus of blog posts. Patricia is a member of The Ontario Poetry Society and the League of Canadian Poets. Completed the 2009 & 2011 November PAD challenges plus 2012 January Challenge with A River of Stones! W E B: Patricia-Anne-McGoldrick   BLOG: PM_Poet   Writer http://www.patricia-anne-mcgoldrick.com/
TWITTER: @pamcgoldrick

Connie L. Peters, originally from western Pennsylvania now lives in Southwest Colorado with her husband, son and two adults with developmental disabilities. Her daughter, also a poet, lives in Arizona. Connie writes fiction, poetry, and creative nonfiction for adults and children. Her poems have been published in Evangel, Cross & Quill, Christian Communicator, Wounded by Words (2008), The Power of Small (2011), Celebrating Christmas (2011), Prompted (2011), The Pagosa Sun, and presedentialprayerteam.com. Hundreds of her articles, devotions, and children's stories have appeared in a variety of publications. She enjoys playing Canasta and Scrabble. She likes to travel and has visited all of the continental United States. Connie has been writing a poem a day since 2004. You can read more of her poetry at http://enthusiaticsoul.blogspot.com/.

Pearl Ketover Prilik, has several published non-fiction books and has been cited, interviewed and excerpted in magazine and newspaper articles on various subjects including parenting and human behavior. PKP, as she is often known online, has been writing poetry since early childhood; during recent years she became a daily active participant at various on-line poetry sites, and at her own poetry blog, "Imagine." She has been published in several online and print poetry venues as well as having several 'micro- stories' published at PostcardShorts.com. Her latest novel is in process of being edited after a kind pass by a major NYC publishing house. With kids grown-up and out, dogs lives well lived and passed, she now enjoys a peaceful quiet home on the South Shore of Long Island with her husband, and an originally tiny feral feline fluff of coal who persistently adopted them. "Dr. Pearl" maintains a private practice as a psychoanalyst, and continues to write poetry, creative fiction and non-fiction on a daily basis. She has recently edited the poetry anthology *Prompted, An International Collection of Poems, (ReallyLoveYourBook, December 2011)*. She is deeply indebted to, and appreciative of, the poets in this anthology for their creative talent and their sparkling individual and collective collaborative supportive spirit.
You can find her blog "Imagine" at: http://drpkp.com/

Meena Rose is a multi-lingual world traveler and transplanted Oregonian; a mother of three children (one boy and two girls) who works as an analyst by day promoting creativity through writing, storytelling and role playing wherever she goes. You can learn more about her through her blog: Through the Eyes of Meena Rose http://meenarose.wordpress.com/.

J.lynn Sheridan once fancied herself a folk singer and has written hundreds of songs and performed them with her guitar in coffee houses, weddings, and bonfires. She graduated from Illinois State University with a degree in Therapeutic Recreation specializing in children with disabilities. Twenty-five years ago, she won a writing contest at a community college with a Shakespearean sonnet and then put her pen down to have babies, homeschool, and assist her husband building his Roofing and Construction business in the Chain O' Lakes area in northern Illinois. Twenty-five years later, she decided it was time to pick up the pen again. She is a graduate of the Christian Writer's Guild Apprenticeship program, has won a few poetry awards, has had several articles published, and has two books drafted, yet poetry will always remain her first literary love. Blog: http://writingonthesun.wordpress.com

Jane Shlensky holds an MFA in creative writing, but has only recently returned to writing poetry and fiction. For thirty-eight years, she taught English at high schools, universities, and community colleges in the U.S. and the People's Republic of China, and after retiring, worked as educational administrator for North Carolina's Teaching Asia Network. A national board certified educator, she served as a board member, conference director, and president of the N.C. English Teachers Association, and was given the North Carolina Outstanding English Teacher award. Her teaching Asian Studies catalyzed her travel throughout Asia and elsewhere on Fulbrights and other study grants and resulted in a growing collection of oddities in art and literature gathered from her excursions. In her spare time, she bakes, makes music, gardens, makes new friends and cherishes old ones, and reads too many books. She makes her home in Bahama, North Carolina with her husband Vladimir and two pushy cats. Her more recent poetry has been published by The Dead Mule School of Southern Literature, Bay Leaves, Writer's Digest, and in Prompted: An International Collection of Poems.

Jay Sizemore has never lived by the sea. He writes poems to separate his voice from the blurred wings of the moth, fading into the silence of the night. His poetry has recently appeared in: the anthology Prompted, on cur.ren.cy, Red River Review, and was featured on Toad the Journal's blog forum. He lives in Nashville, TN, with his wife Elizabeth. They have three cats.

Marian Veverka has spent most of her life on the shores of Lake Erie. Born in Cleveland, she married and moved to Marblehead OH where she still resides. She and her husband had a mini farm including large gardens and chickens. They raised 6 children. When her children were older, Marian studied Creative Writing at Bowling Green State University and received her BFA. She also spent 2 years at the University of Kentucky before her marriage. She writes poetry, short stories, creative non-fiction and has written 2 novels, unpublished. Recently, her poems have appeared in "A Prairie Journal", "Moondance" Magazine, "Pirene's Fountain", "Up the Staircase". "Main Channel voices", "Occupy Poetry" "Smoking Magazine" and "Festival of the Trees." A poem "A Grandchild Turns Two" is included in "Bigger Than they Appear", an anthology of very short poems. Marian worked in the Port Clinton library and is now retired after 30 some years. She enjoys reading and keeping up with current events .
Marian's blog is Marianv.blog.co.uk

Rosemary Nissen-Wade is a widely-published Australian poet who has also had short fiction and articles published. Once best known as a dynamic performance poet, in recent years she has embraced online sharing of her work in blogs, e-publications and international poetry groups. She is a co-administrator of the 'Haiku on Friday', 'Tanka on Tuesday' and 'Free Verse Weekends' groups on Facebook, and writes the 'I Wish I'd Written This' series at Poets United: http://poetryblogroll.blogspot.com.au. She is a teacher of creative writing who has worked in a variety of venues from tertiary colleges to maximum security prisons, and currently at a local Neighbourhood Centre. She also works as a proof-reader and copy-editor. In the eighties and nineties she was an independent poetry publisher, as proprietor of Abalone Press and as one of the Pariah Press Cooperative. Her latest (printed) book is Secret Leopard: New and Selected Poems 1974-2005 (Alyscamps Press) available from Amazon, and from the author through her blogs and website. (Her previous hard copy collections, Universe Cat and Small Poems of April, are now out of print.) She is presently putting together a series of chapbooks as eBooks. As well as a poet, she is a Reiki Master and a professional psychic medium. She holds a Bachelor of Arts degree from the University of Melbourne (1962)

Rosemary's main poetry blog is The Passionate Crone: http://passionatecrone.blogspot.com/ where links can be found to the other three.

Her personal blog is SnakyPoet: http://rosemary-nissen-wade.blogspot.com/

Her website, shared with her writer husband Andrew Wade, is Life Magic http://www.nissen-wade.com

Richard Walker, a.k.a. Mr. Walker, is originally from Indiana, but currently lives in California. He teaches in a public elementary school in San Francisco, and lives in a suburb south of the city with his wife and their two sons. As a teacher, he enjoys working with California Poets in the Schools, and does his best to bring poetry into his classroom as often as he is able. Many years ago, in his college days, he had a poem published in a student anthology, but that is his sole publication thus far. He blogs at Sadly Waiting for Recess, which is named after a former student's poem; in November, he posts how he is doing with his novel writing, as he participates in National Novel Writing Month. You will find his blog at http://sadlywaiting.wordpress.com.

A note from the editor:

And yet we laugh

And yet we laugh
And sing and toss
Off our shoes and
Dance barefoot on
Aquamarine shores
Jiggling babies of hope
On strong hips
Built for bearing

pkp

www.ingramcontent.com/pod-product-compliance
Lightning Source LLC
Chambersburg PA
CBHW031547040426
42452CB00006B/229